DEC 14

D006027

ACROSS

1 Rewrite items in New Yo newspaper (5)

4 Crossword dictionary rooms (8)

8 Cycles back to video game company (4)

9 Revolutionary force almost mad at infamous Spanish torturer (10)

10 West of Italy's capital, politico Sarah (Democrat) with mom or dad (10)

11 Name in the middle of caricatures! (4)

12 Get up around noon and gargle (5)

14 British dirty old man by the French yard where the Enigma code was broken (9)

17 Swung a fist (missing the head) getting a wallop in and split (9)

20 Crossword inventor's success in speech (5)

21 Yours truly and an alien come face-to-face (4)

23 Puzzle dragged on, enveloping confused Republican squad (4, 6)

26 Puzzle editor to be paid to sell imperfections to the Reverend (4, 6)

27 Excellent shot goes out (4)

28 Mandator meandering without rhyme or reason (2, 6)

29 Highly polished Southern rock guitar line (5)

1 ...n, NPR venue covers brooding one for left-leaning magazine (3, 6)

2 Note a Michigan city for snowbirds (5)

3 Overstuffed engagements after switching first and last (5)

4 Lewis who wrote Christmas song for audition (7)

5 Most intense Western Indians appear in part of play (7)

6 Every nine weeks: BLT, hominy, bananas (9)

7 "Way cool, using deadly gas!" (5)

13 Tiny amount of interest in Lily-like flower (9)

14 Pedestrian left out nuts (3)

15 After the face off, bow to pressure and then stop (3)

16 Hungarian puzzle maker and I broke urn, sadly (4, 5)

18 Mob lacking resistance around her bovine abode (7)

19 Accidentally murder a contributor to the *Listener*? (7)

22 Cited wrong statute (5)

24 Takes a direction from forces for kings and queens, say (5)

25 Selection of charcuterie for child development centers? (5)

THE CROSSWORD CENTURY

THE CROSSWORD CENTURY

100 YEARS OF WITTY WORDPLAY, INGENIOUS PUZZLES, AND LINGUISTIC MISCHIEF

ALAN CONNOR

GOTHAM BOOKS

GOTHAM BOOKS
Published by the Penguin Group
Penguin Group (USA) LLC
375 Hudson Street
New York, New York 10014

USA | Canada | UK | Ireland | Australia | New Zealand | India | South Africa | China
penguin.com
A Penguin Random House Company

Copyright © 2014 by Alan Connor

Photograph Credits
Page 54, top: Reprinted with permission from Editions Fayard
Page 54, bottom: Reprinted with permission from David R. Godine
Page 66: Courtesy of Jeremiah Farrell
Page 110: © ITV Global/The Kobal Collection
Page 170: Courtesy of Calendar Puzzles

Penguin supports copyright. Copyright fuels creativity, encourages diverse voices, promotes free speech, and creates a vibrant culture. Thank you for buying an authorized edition of this book and for complying with copyright laws by not reproducing, scanning, or distributing any part of it in any form without permission. You are supporting writers and allowing Penguin to continue to publish books for every reader.

Gotham Books and the skyscraper logo are trademarks of Penguin Group (USA) LLC.

LIBRARY OF CONGRESS CATALOGING-IN-PUBLICATION DATA
Connor, Alan.
The crossword century : 100 years of witty wordplay, ingenious puzzles, and linguistic mischief / Alan Connor.
pages cm
Includes index.
ISBN 978-1-59240-858-0 (hardcover)
1. Crossword puzzles—History. I. Title.
GV1507.C7C544 2014
793.73'2—dc23 2014002612

Printed in the United States of America
1 3 5 7 9 10 8 6 4 2

Set in Adobe Caslon • Designed by Elke Sigal

While the author has made every effort to provide accurate telephone numbers, Internet addresses, and other contact information at the time of publication, neither the publisher nor the author assumes any responsibility for errors or for changes that occur after publication. Further, the publisher does not have any control over and does not assume any responsibility for author or third-party websites or their content.

FOR LUCY

CONTENTS

INTRODUCTION ix

PART ONE

ACROSS

GENESIS 3
FAD 13
JARGON 20
ANCESTORS 22
NINA 30
FAIR 36
WICKED 40
ALAMO 43
AUTHORSHIP 49
TRANSLATION 52
CANT 56
NEWS 61
SPOONER 68
SONDHEIM 76
CRYPTIC 79

PART TWO

DOWN

DOUBLE-CROSSING 91
GAGA 97
FAST 103
ADDICTION 109
DUAL 113
PROGRAM 118
INTELLIGENCE 125
GUMSHOE 133
SIMPSON 139
BUG 145
PLUM 153
A-LIST 160
FUTURE 162
IMPLEMENT 172

RESOURCES 175
ACKNOWLEDGMENTS 179
INDEX 181
PUZZLE SOLUTION 192

INTRODUCTION

This is a book about having FUN with words. And if you're wondering why that word is in capital letters, all will become clear.

And it's a very particular form of fun with words: one that involves jumbling and tumbling them into eye-pleasingly symmetrical patterns and making riddles, jokes, and poetry in the form of crossword clues. A love of crosswords is also a love of language—albeit a love that enjoys seeing the object of its affections toyed with, tickled, and flipped upside down.

Crossword puzzles are a silly, playful way of taking English and making it into a game. They have been doing so since December 21, 1913, when the world's first crossword appeared—although lovers of language had been deriving pleasure from wordplay long before then, of course. However, it was the crossword that came to supersede all other puzzles. It has become a cornerstone of almost all newspapers and, for many, a fondly anticipated daily appointment.

The crossword today looks quite different than that first puzzle—or that should perhaps read "crosswords today" so as to encompass the baroque creations seen in Sunday papers, the strange mutant British form known as the cryptic, and all of the themed and jokey variants on offer on any given day.

What they have in common is the pleasure of identifying what the constructor is asking for and seeing the answers mesh with one another until the puzzle is finished. For a century, the worker has whiled away journeys and parents have passed on tips and tricks in the hope that each grid tackled will be correctly filled.

In *The Crossword Century*, we'll be looking at the playfulness, the humor, and the frustration of the crossword in all its forms, and how the world of the puzzle has overlapped with espionage and humor, current affairs and literature. We'll see fictional crossword encounters, from *The West Wing* to *The Simpsons*, and we'll see crosswords from the real world: the one that seemed to predict the outcome of a presidential election and the ones that appeared to be giving away the secrets of the Second World War.

We'll look at how clues tantalize those who are addicted to puzzles by sending the solver on wild-goose chases, by being sweetly silly and soberly serious, and by stubbornly withholding their real meanings until the penny drops.

And we ask questions about the experience of solving: Why do some people try to finish crosswords as quickly as possible? Can computers crack clues? And does puzzling really stave off dementia?

As for how to read this book, please feel free to treat it like a puzzle. That is to say, you can start at 1 across and work sequentially, or you can dive in and out and follow your instincts. The chapters are in two sections: The ACROSS entries look at the creation of puzzles and the strange things that can go on within clues and grids, while the DOWNs describe what happens to the crossword once it escapes into the world and meets its solvers.

Like the British man who created the first crossword in New York, we'll be crossing the Atlantic Ocean—a few times, in fact—and I humbly hope that along the way I might persuade you that the baffling-looking British cryptic is a lot more enjoyable than legend has it.

Are you ready for FUN?

PART ONE

ACROSS

FALL IN A GARDEN, DEPICTED?

GENESIS

How the crossword first appeared in 1913 and became an overnight sensation in 1924

N*ewsday*'s crossword editor puts it best. "Liverpool's two greatest gifts to the world of popular culture," writes Stanley Newman, "are the Beatles and Arthur Wynne."

The comparison with the Beatles is on the money—or, to use a more British locution, spot-on. Like the music of the Fab Four, the crossword is a global phenomenon that is at once American and British. But while the Beatles are known wherever recorded music is played, Arthur Wynne's name remains unspoken by almost all. Who was he?

Well, he wasn't the Lennon or the McCartney of crosswords; we'll meet them soon enough. He was perhaps crosswords' Fats Domino: a pioneer who would see his innovation taken by others to strange, often baroque mutant forms and variants.

Not that this was how Wynne saw his career playing out when he became one of the forty million people who emigrated from Europe between 1830 and 1930, and one of the nine million heading from Liverpool for the New World during that same period.

The son of the editor of *The Liverpool Mercury*, Wynne was—at least initially, and in his own mind—a journalist. He spent most of his newspaper career working for the empire of print mogul William Randolph Hearst. His legacy, though, was not a piece of reporting, and it appeared in the New York *World*, a Democrat-supporting daily published by Hearst's rival, Joseph Pulitzer.

As a kind of precursor to the *New York Post*, *The World* mixed sensation with investigation, and it was Wynne's job to add puzzles to the jokes and cartoons for "Fun," the Sunday magazine section. He had messed around with tried-and-tested formats: word searches, mazes, anagrams, rebuses.

Another available template was something called the word square, which we will look at in more detail in a later chapter. It takes up space, a very desirable property if you're in charge of "Fun." It asks the reader to think of answers. But it's very limited. Imagine a crossword in which each answer appears twice in the grid: once as an across and again as a down. Very pleasing in terms of visual symmetry—whether foursquare square or tilted, as word squares often were, to make a diamond—but there are only so many words that fit with one another in this way.

It's also a less demanding challenge for the solver: In a four-by-four word square, say, as soon as the first four-letter word goes in, once across and once down, the grid is 44 percent filled.

For the Christmas edition of the New York *World* on Sunday, December 21, 1913, Wynne tried something new. What if the entries read differently across and down? And so, without fanfare, this:

Fill in the small squares with words which agree with the following definitions.

2-3.	What bargain hunters enjoy.
6-22.	What we all should be.
4-5.	A written acknowledgment.
4-26.	A day dream.
6-7.	Such and nothing more.
2-11.	A talon.
10-11.	A bird.

19-28. A pigeon.
14-15. Opposed to less.
F-7. Part of your head.
18-19. What this puzzle is.
23-30. A river in Russia.
22-23. An animal of prey.
1-32. To govern.
26-27. The close of a day.
33-34. An aromatic plant.
28-29. To elude.
N-8. A fist.
30-31. The plural of is.
24-31. To agree with.
8-9. To cultivate.
3-12. Part of a ship.
12-13. A bar of wood or iron.
20-29. One.
16-17. What artists learn to do.
5-27. Exchanging.
20-21. Fastened.
9-25. To sink in mud.
24-25. Found on the seashore.
13-21. A boy.
10-18. The fiber of the gomuti palm.

The answers are in the Resources section at the end of this book. Puzzles nowadays don't come with an instruction to "fill in the small squares" and would be more likely to clue DOH with a reference to Homer Simpson than by "Fiber of the gomuti palm," but it's recognizably a crossword. Or, rather, a "Word-Cross." Wynne's name is just as good a way of describing the pastime as the more familiar version, but a typographical anomaly two weeks later offered the alternative "Find the Missing Cross Words." The following week's heading announced a "Cross-Word Puzzle," and that's the version that stuck. It was to be some decades later that the name decisively shed its fussy capitals and sporadic hyphen.

It includes one answer twice (DOVE), and the clue for MIRED is—what's a polite word here?—misleading, but there it is: a new thing in the world. The most important thing about the first puzzle is that big "FUN" across the second row. It might have been there because it was the name of the Sunday supplement, but it also served as a manifesto for crosswording. Individual puzzles may or may not be edifying, challenging, or distracting, but they must always be fun. After all, nobody is forcing solvers to look at them.

The second most important thing is the squares. The crossword's antecedent, the double acrostic (again, see below), tended to offer only the clues: The solver put the answers together in his or her head, or found somewhere to write the letters. But twentieth-century printing technology made it easier to offer a grid depiction of the problem that was both clearer and more enticing, the little boxes staring up from the newsprint, begging to be filled.

The prewar period was one of linguistic innovation and reinvention. We will look at spoonerisms below. This was also a world that saw innovations with language: entirely new creations, such as the artificial languages Esperanto and Ido, and different means of conveying words, such as developments in stenography. And then there was the crossword, which broke up language into abstract units for reassembly: Rising newspaper sales and the age of mechanical reproduction helped to make the puzzle the most widely disseminated way of messing around with words. Even with the reader-compiled puzzles that occasionally took the place of Wynne's in *The World*, though, it remained only a weekly phenomenon, and for the first ten years of its life it existed exclusively as an American phenomenon—indeed, it existed solely within the pages of that one newspaper. The puzzle had its devotees, but nobody spotted its potential until the faddish twenties arrived.

It became known to millions more in that decade when it started appearing outside *The World*—and not in other papers but in books. On January 2, 1924, the aspiring publisher Dick Simon went for supper with his aunt Wixie, who asked him where she could get a book of Cross-Words for a niece who had become addicted to the puzzles in *The World*. Simon mentioned the query to his would-be business partner, Lincoln Schuster, and they discovered that no such book existed.

On the one hand, this was good news: They had formed a publishing company but so far had no manuscripts to publish. On the other, their aspirations for Simon & Schuster were considerably higher than a collection of trivia(l) puzzles. The compromise was a corporate alias named after their telephone exchange: Plaza Publishing.

The next difficulty was getting the puzzles. As a first step Simon and Schuster approached not Wynne but one of his subordinates. Margaret Petherbridge had been appointed as a sub-editor by *The World* in 1920; being both young and a woman, she was assigned the suitably lowly task of fact-checking the crosswords to try to reduce the volume of letters of complaint (of which more later), and now found her intended career in journalism permanently on hold.

Petherbridge was offered an advance of $25 to assemble enough puzzles for a book. Simon and Schuster decided to attach a sharpened pencil to every copy, priced it at $1.35, and spent their remaining prelaunch money on a one-inch ad in the New York *World*. Their campaign pushed the idea that the crossword was the Next Big Thing:

1921—Coué
1922—Mah Jong
1923—Bananas
1924—THE CROSS WORD PUZZLE BOOK

Long-shot business ventures rarely end well—the typical results are penury and shame. But the stories of failure are not often told, and this is not one of them. This is one of those familiar but wholly anomalous stories of unlikely triumph—where a bookseller friend of Simon buys twenty-five copies as a gesture of friendship but has to order thousands more; where *The World*'s top columnist, Franklin P. Adams, had predicted that Simon and Schuster would "lose their shirts," only to start a piece four months later with the announcement: "Hooray! Hooray! Hooray! Hooray! *The Cross-Word Puzzle Book* is out today."

It is also a story where:

- each of the four collections published that year topped the nonfiction bestseller list

- the second edition, priced at a more modest 25¢, received from the keenest of the distributors an order for 250,000 copies—then unprecedented in book publishing

- Simon & Schuster's crossword compilations became the longest continuously published book series

It was the making of one of the major world publishers, and as rival firms produced their own puzzle series, it was excellent news for publishing in general—especially as, unlike pesky authors producing books of fiction or non-, crossword constructors would work for little or even no pay. The only downside for publishers was a side effect of the fierce competition: In case of low sales, Simon & Schuster offered to take back unsold crossword collections from bookshops, thereby instigating the practice of "returns," very beneficial to megachains but increasing the element of risk for publishers ever since.

It was also the making of the crossword. The most intense interest in crosswords ever was in midtwenties America, and was largely centered on books of puzzles. It was only later that the newspaper reclaimed its status as the default home of the crossword. However, perhaps even more important than the number of solvers solving was the way the form matured. In 1926 Margaret Petherbridge had taken the name Farrar following her marriage to John C. Farrar, founder of another publishing giant, Farrar, Straus and Giroux. As Margaret Farrar, she tidied up the messy conventions of crosswording: She may have become involved with puzzling by chance, but she thought deeply and effectively about what made one crossword better than another.

Modern-day solvers (or "solutionists," as they were sometimes described in the twenties) baffled by Wynne's system for numbering clues have Farrar to thank for the cleaner "1 across" format, saving them, across a lifetime of solving, hours lost to tracing and connecting "F," say, to "7." Her preference for answers of at least three letters makes for a more satisfying experience, and the aesthetics she proposed for the grid are now characteristic of all puzzles (with the exception of some of the more willfully experimental examples we will meet along the way in this book).

Margaret Farrar's parameters for an aesthetically pleasing grid are symmetry, a minimum letter-count of three in answers, and "all-over interlock"—in layman's speak, the grid does not have separate sections and the solver can travel from any part of it to another.

Farrar's ingenuity was finally rewarded in 1942 when she became *The New York Times*'s first crossword editor. Wynne had quietly retired in 1918 and died in Clearwater, Florida, in 1945. When the first crosswords appeared, he had wished to patent the format. Lacking the necessary funds for the process, however, he asked *The World* to contribute and was told by business manager F. D. White and assistant manager F. D. Carruthers that "it was just one of those puzzle fads that people would get tired of within six months." In 1925, he did, however, obtain a patent for “an improvement or variation of the well-known cross word puzzle” in which the cells formed a kind of rhombus. Sadly, for him, it never took off.

Yet we crossword lovers should be very glad that Wynne failed to “own” the crossword. Even if such a claim were enforceable, given the puzzle’s obvious debt to earlier diversions, it is precisely the freedom of the format and the deviations from its original structure that have made crosswords such a rich format and such a satisfying pastime. Had the crossword been patented, it would indeed have been quickly forgotten and filed under “obsolete wordplay,” between the clerihew and the cryptarithm.

(The clerihew, by the by, was a form of comic verse that contained the name of a well-known person. And the cryptarithm, also known as the alphametic, was a mathematical puzzle in which an arithmetical proposition has its numbers replaced by letters. Neither, so far as I know, ever achieved sufficient popularity to be rendered in the form of cookies, earrings, or novelty songs. Unlike . . .)

FAD

How Americans celebrated the crossword—but the British were not so sure

In 1920s America, fads were quite the vogue. Flappers had the Charleston, the stock market had dangerous overspeculation, and it seemed that everyone had the crossword. The very look of a crossword grid was, for a while, chic: Black-and-white squares adorned earrings, dresses, and collar pins, and it was reported that checked patterns in general had never been in such demand.

The most opulent manifestation of the craze was a Broadway revue, *Puzzles of 1925*, which features a scene in a crossword puzzle sanatorium filled with those driven to madness by clueing fever. Its lyrics echoed the papers' concern about home wrecking: "The house has gone to ruin / Since all that Mother's doin' / Is putting letters in the little squares." At the same time, various songwriters used crosswords as romantic analogy: "Cross

Words Between My Sweetie and Me" by the Little Ramblers and "Crossword Mama You're Puzzling Me" by Papalia & His Orchestra, not to mention "Cross Word Papa (You Sure Puzzle Me)" by Josie Miles.

Crosswords began to appear in the most unlikely areas of public life: Puzzle competitions between Yale and Harvard were to be expected, perhaps less so those between New York's fire brigade and police department before packed houses at Wanamaker's Auditorium.

The church was not immune, as seen by witnesses of the celebrated incidence of the Reverend George McElveen of Pittsburgh, who rendered a sermon in the form of a puzzle and asked worshippers to solve the clues before the preaching began.

The British, too, caught on, though not without a fight from the nation's moral guardians. The first crossword in a British publication appeared quietly in February 1922, in *Pearson's Magazine*. More appeared over the next few years, but these tended to be found in books, not in newspapers. It was not just that the papers were slow to see the puzzle's appeal; they were actively hostile to the very notion of the crossword.

They warned nervous citizens of the damage this scourge was already doing to American citizens. In December 1924 an editorial in the London *Times* had the chilling headline AN ENSLAVED AMERICA. The crossword, it explained, "has grown from the pastime of a few ingenious idlers into a national institution: a menace because it is making devastating inroads on the working hours of every rank of society." Solvers could, it seemed, be seen "quite shamelessly" staring at their grids, morning, noon, and night . . .

. . . cudgeling their brains for a four-letter word meaning "molten rock" or a six-letter word meaning "idler," or what not: in trains and trams, or omnibuses, in subways, in private offices and counting-rooms, in factories and homes, and even—although as yet rarely—with hymnals for camouflage, in church.

The choice of "idler" as an example of a clue is not, I suspect, an idle one. As with video games and recreational drugs, crosswords alarmed the self-appointed defenders of morality because people who are solving a crossword are simply enjoying themselves. Five million man-hours, warned the London *Times*'s New York correspondent, were being lost every day as workers forgot their duty to contribute to the gross national product, lost in the pure pleasure of finding synonyms.

And because of this, the *Tamworth Herald* reported in the same year, pernicious puzzles "have been known to break up homes." This family wrecking comes about when husbands spend time solving a clue rather than earning a crust. The solution of one concerned policeman was to enforce on addicts a ration of three puzzles a day, with ten days' imprisonment if a fourth was attempted.

In February 1925 the London *Times* announced that crosswords had, with "the speed of a meteorological depression," crossed the Atlantic. "The nation still stands before the blast," the paper thunders, "and no man can say it will stand erect again." Prepare yourself for some mayhem.

"The damage caused to dictionaries in the library at Wimbledon by people doing cross-word puzzles," we read later that year, "has been so great that the committee has withdrawn all the volumes." Across the capital, in Willesden, it was the same sad story. Dulwich Library, meanwhile, started blacking out the white squares of crossword grids with a heavy pencil, "to prevent any one person from keeping a newspaper for more than a reasonable length of time."

Those selfish paper-hogging solvers! Meanwhile, booksellers bemoaned falling sales of the novel—no longer itself considered a menace to society—in favor of "dictionaries, glossaries, dictionaries of synonyms, &c." The *Nottingham Evening Post* went on:

> *The picture theaters are also complaining that cross-words keep people at home. They get immersed in a problem and forget all about Gloria Swanson, Lillian Gish, and the other stars of the film constellation.*

And it gets worse. In another part of Nottingham—poor puzzle-blighted Nottingham—the zookeeper was swamped in correspondence. The reason? Crosswords, of course. He listed some of the inquiries that were keeping him from his animals:

> *What is a word of three letters meaning a female swan? What is a female kangaroo, or a fragile creature in six letters ending in TO?*

(That would be PEN, DOE, and . . . I'm not sure. There's a mackerel-like fish called the BONITO . . . ?) Meantime, across town at the theater, the stage was bare because one Mr. Matheson Lang, absorbed in a puzzle, had missed his entrance. "This caused him much chagrin," reported the local press, "for he is extremely conscientious as regards his stage work."

Who was safe from this funk? Surely the world of grocery was unblighted? Apparently not:

> *A girl asked a busy grocer to name the different brands of flour he kept. When he had done so, expecting a sale, she said she didn't want to buy any. She just thought one of the names might fit into a cross-word puzzle she was doing.*

Worrying stuff. Happily for society at large, the crossword was soon to find itself pursued by the law. Prizes had started appearing for puzzles—another symptom of the something-for-nothing culture, tutted the London *Times*—along with a new variant on the crossword that would seem very unfamiliar to the solver of today.

By the end of 1926 the *News of the World*, *The People*, the *Daily Sketch*, and the *Sunday Graphic* were among the papers to print prize crosswords, which were not only "pay-to-play" but had multiple clues for which there was more than one correct answer.

The grids contained far more black squares than normal grids—the reason for which became clear when you reached a clue such as "You look forward to getting this when you are in hospital." Solvers who hoped that their choice between BETTER and LETTER would be decided by a B or an L in another clue found that there was no such other clue. The crucial squares stood alone. If you did manage to complete the grid correctly, a prize was offered—but those ambiguities ensured that the number of "correct" entries for each puzzle would be tiny.

The immense popularity of these puzzles made them very lucrative for the syndicates and newspapers that created them, and court summons were issued by the police, who insisted that the puzzles were not crosswords at all but thinly disguised lotteries. A lawyer for the police argued at London's top magistrates' court that "the words are ridiculously easy, and a child of 12 should have no difficulty in solving them." At times it seemed that the crossword itself was on trial: Thanks to the Betting and Lotteries Bill, it became literally as well as morally criminal.

However, the genuine crossword benefited in invidious comparison: As the judges shut down the lotteries, the puzzle survived. Indeed, the crossword was on the way to becoming respectable. The London *Telegraph* had started publishing one on July 30, 1925, and by the end of the decade, the London *Times* had started to wonder if these puzzles weren't so bad after all. Or, in the words of BBC correspondent Martin Bell, whose father was the London *Times*'s first constructor, the paper "was losing circulation hand-over-fist to the *Telegraph* because the *Telegraph* had the new-fangled American fashion, the crossword, so the *Times* had to get one pretty sharpish."

The motivation might have been financial and the about-face a tad hypocritical after all the scaremongering, but the appearance on February 1, 1930, of a puzzle in the paper with the slogan "Top People take *The Times*" marked the crossword's move to unambiguous respectability. Soon *The Spectator* and *The Listener* followed, and the British press began to rely on puzzles for a good, and indisputable, proportion of its newsstand sales, as some readers would buy a copy, have a bash at the crossword, then throw the paper away unread.

When that first constructor for the London *Times*, Adrian Bell, was told by his own father that he would be constructing puzzles, he replied, "But Father, I haven't even solved a crossword puzzle," only to be told, "Well, you've got just ten days to learn!" Bell learned fast and went on to write such well-loved clues as "Die of cold? (3,4)" and "Spoils of War (4)."

(Answers in the chapter FAIR. But first there is a whole new language to master . . .)

INSIDE BASEBALL'S LANGUAGE?

JARGON

The metaphors of the crossword puzzle

When the crossword first appeared, its mechanics were described in detail that is tediously verbose to today's solver. Indeed, Arthur Wynne did not speak of "grids" or even "clues" ("Fill in the small squares with words which agree with the following definitions") since the vocabulary of crosswording had yet to evolve.

Even "grid," in the sense of the lines on maps and diagrams, did not appear until the First World War, which means that it was not really available as a way of describing the layout of the first puzzles. And it's a grisly metaphor, too: The real-life gridiron was a lattice-shaped arrangement of metal bars useful for griddling food—or torturing people. But perhaps, if you're stuck on a Sunday afternoon with an especially tricky southeastern corner of your grid unfilled, the metaphor is apt.

There's another instrument of torture in the word "crossword" itself: the cross, from which we get the sense of going side to side denoted by "across." (Conversely, Old English speakers called a hill a "dúne" and used "of dúne" to refer to the direction you take when leaving the top of one; from this we got "down," a word still used to describe hills and slopes in some parts of the United Kingdom.)

Likewise analogous is "clue." In the fourteenth century, a clue was a ball of thread. Those balls are useful for finding your way out of mazes both literal (kudos, Theseus) and metaphorical: The Elizabethan poet Michael Drayton bemoaned "loosing the clew which led us safely in," leaving him "lost within this Labyrinth of lust." Later, you didn't need the maze as part of the metaphor, and might use the word in the context of detection: In Charlotte Brontë's *Shirley*, Caroline Helstone announces that "I have a clue to the identity of one, at least, of the men who broke my frames."

Finally, a crypt can be an underground hiding place or a vault in a church—or, if you're the subject of religious persecution, both simultaneously. Francis Bacon used "cryptic" as a noun to describe communication using secret methods; Agatha Christie used it as an adjective when the meaning of some words or behavior is not immediately apparent: a problem if you're trying to solve a murder, but all part of the fun if the solving is of the puzzling kind.

(Before the crossword, there was another "cross"-sounding puzzle, though this one took its name from the Greek *ἄκρο*—meaning "extreme." Welcome to the crossword's forefather, the baffling double acrostic . . .)

RELATIVES WHO ARE REPEATEDLY GREAT?

ANCESTORS

The prehistory of wordplay

The double acrostic was a wholly respectable way of whiling away an evening in Victorian England—so respectable, and so Victorian, that those who were addicted to the puzzles claimed that Queen Victoria herself both solved and constructed them.

Here is one attributed to her majesty. It was supposedly a gift "for the royal children," whose job as solvers was to give each clue an answer such that their first letters, read top to bottom, spelled out a place name, and the last letters, bottom to top, what that place was famous for:

A city in Italy
A river in Germany
A town in the United States

A town in North America
A town in Holland
The Turkish name of Constantinople
A town in Bothnia
A city in Greece
A circle on the globe

Got it yet?

NapleS
ElbE
WashingtoN
CincinnatI
AmsterdaM
StambouL
TorneA
LepantO
EclipticC

So, the first letters give us NEWCASTLE—not the city in Oklahoma, or any of the Newcastles in Texas, Washington, and Wyoming, but the northern English city so famous for its COALMINES (to be found in the last letters) that the British expression "to carry coals to Newcastle" is shorthand for doing something unnecessary.

The apparent imprimatur of the sovereign may have helped to popularize the double acrostic, but her influence was as nothing compared to that of the age of mechanical reproduction. In the mid-nineteenth century, the puzzles began to appear in *The*

Illustrated London News, constructed by the clergyman and humorist Cuthbert Bede, author of *The Adventures of Mr. Verdant Green*.

His double acrostics became a national craze. Marion Spielmann's 1895 history of *Punch* tells how Bede received letters about his puzzles from all over the world, "forwarded to him in packets by rail." In America, the convoluted acrostic was more of a poet's game, as seen in the intricate creations of Edgar Allan Poe, but the puzzle variant would have been familiar to one Arthur Wynne when, in New York in 1913, he found himself in need of a new kind of puzzle.

The grip of the acrostic may be hard to credit today, when such wordplay appears seldom outside of the occasional British-style cryptic clue, but a story by Vladimir Nabokov hints at the revelatory power once possessed by this form of wordplay. In the final paragraph of 1951's "The Vane Sisters," the narrator unknowingly reveals that the two dead women of the title have been affecting his experiences, even leaving a message in acrostic form in his own writing. Nabokov wrote that this otherworldly device could "only be tried once in a thousand years of fiction," but his choice of Sybil as the name for one of the Vanes makes a link that goes back to classical antiquity.

The first acrostics to bear the name were the prophecies of the Erythraean Sibyl, a prophetess who wrote verses on leaves that could be rearranged such that the initial letters conveyed some important message. They were, however, sometimes a little obscure. Acrostics create readability obstacles sometimes: troubles in comprehensibility.

The habit of leaving hidden messages in the first letters of verses can also be found in the Hebrew version of the Old Testament, Latin poems, and the runes of the Anglo-Saxon poet Cynewulf.

For none of these protopuzzlers was the acrostic merely a bit of fun. Leaving behind our everyday assumption that for any word or sentence there is a single, graspable sense involves accepting that there is an invisible sense—and before these were put there by other humans in the pursuit of entertainment, they were thought to be indicative of some more cosmic truths.

Take the simplest form of mucking about with words: the anagram. In the ancient world, if one word could be jumbled to make another, it was thought, there had to be a reason. Such was the thinking of many ancient prophets, who, writes the anthropologist Marcel Danesi, "were essentially anagrammatists who interpreted this heavenly form of language." If anagrams were a means of obtaining information sent by a higher power, then being good at solving them made you a soothsayer.

If you could give the king a bunch of anagrams of the names of the members of his court, he might well think you'd found a way of revealing their innermost characters and intentions, and your prize for being good at jumbling letters would be gold.

What we think of nowadays as a "clue" was likewise a more potent challenge. When *The New York Times* uses "Big piece of crust?" to elicit CONTINENT, the intention is to describe the answer while appearing to depict something completely different. The legendary Sphinx did much the same when it demanded of its Greek victims: "Which creature walks on four legs in the morning, two legs in the afternoon, and three legs in the evening?"

The answer is MAN, who starts life crawling and ends up with a cane. The jeopardy was greater when the Sphinx asked you a question: You'd be strangled if you got it wrong, rather than leaving some gaps at 13 across; even Oedipus, who got it right, received as part of his prize marriage to a woman who turned out to be his mother, so it was really a lose-lose proposition. But the sly humor is the same as that exhibited by today's constructors.

Those constructors need somewhere to put their clues, and for that, we need to look at the palindrome—the trick where a phrase reads the same backward as it does forward. Not easy to construct; so tricky, in fact, that it helped to be Lord of Evil Arts to manage it. Here's a pair of Satan's, cited by Étienne Tabourot in 1585:

Signa, te Signa; temere me tangis et angis;
Roma tibi subito motibus ibit amor.

This complaint is addressed to Saint Martin, who has ordered the devil to change into a donkey and carry him to Rome. It translates as "Cross, cross thyself; thou plaguest and vexest me without necessity; for, owing to my exertions, thou wilt soon reach Rome, the object of thy wishes."

Terrifying. However, when they're not being hurled at you by the Prince of Darkness, multiword palindromes like the above can be giddyingly captivating.

And that urge to travel simultaneously in two directions predates Saint Martin. The same ROMA . . . AMOR palindrome has its most beautiful physical manifestation in Pompeii.

There, those two words form part of a design that is the link between the palindrome and the crossword: the word square. Carved into the wall of the Domus Poppaeorum is:

R O M A
O L I M
M I L O
A M O R

What does it mean? Nobody knows. Perhaps the "Milo" lines are a tribute to the sixth-century-BC athlete Milo of Croton, who could carry an adult ox on his shoulders. That's a guess. Whatever the significance of each component, there's no argument about the grace with which they fit together. Even more impressive is:

S A T O R
A R E P O
T E N E T
O P E R A
R O T A S

It's a palindrome all right, and this time it has a plausible meaning—"the sower, Arepo, skillfully guides the wheels"—that lends itself better than Roma, Milo, etc., to interpretation, particularly if you allow yourself a bit of wiggle room. If Arepo is God and the wheels are metaphorical, too, the square would convey that the big guy upstairs has his eye on all of creation.

There are a few problems with this. One is that the God interpretation is wholly metaphorical and so equally valid would be any paraphrase where Someone skillfully does Something to Something Else. The second problem is that the canny Roman who devised the square may have invented the letter string AREPO to make the whole thing work, a compromise familiar to many constructors.

But to quibble is to miss the point. Like the anagram, the word square persisted as a source of fascination: If words could be made to fit together so well, the reason had to be a good one, and probably divine. Sure enough, if you stare at the Sator word square, truths reveal themselves: You can anagram the twenty-five letters into a plausible prayer, or find two instances of the first two words of the Lord's prayer, PATER NOSTER, crossing on the N.

And even if you don't see divine intervention, you have to marvel at the symmetry. Or, perhaps, see whether you can construct one yourself.

By the nineteenth and early twentieth century, various minds applied themselves to devising plausible squares of greater size. Word squares could be found in Victorian newspapers and magazines. Sometimes the letters were removed and readers provided with, effectively, a blank grid and clues for the words that ought to fill it. The word diamond was a popular variant, and it's not hard to see the tiny evolutionary leap from that type of puzzle to the first crossword, Arthur Wynne's "Word-Cross."

(Finding hidden messages, then, does not have to reveal the divine to be of value. Stripped of their metaphysics and rendered through Victorian mechanical reproduction, these devices still offer up that moment of revelation—but purely for fun. A little bit of magic, literally boxed up for daily consumption in the quotidian wrapping of newspaper. Though, of course, the secret messages are still there . . .)

NINA

When crosswords contain more than just the answers to the clues

In 1945 a daughter was born to the caricaturist Al Hirschfeld. She was named Nina. From that day, he concealed the letters of his daughter's name somewhere in most of his drawings. The letters N, I, N, and A are wholly inessential to your enjoyment of any of his cartoons but lie there as a treat, woven into someone's hair or the folds of his or her clothing, if you know what you're looking for—much like Alfred Hitchcock's cameos, which can be seen in almost all of his films.

"Ninas" is a more charming term than "alfreds" and lives on as a way of describing hidden extra elements that can be discovered in completed crossword grids. Like their near namesakes, ninjas, ninas operate in the shadows. They're not part of the solve, but they raise a smile on the faces of those who spot them.

They can be found—if you know where to look—in British "concise" crosswords, which are a kind of pared-down cousin of the American style. Relying almost solely on straight definitions, they are nonetheless constructed by the same warped minds who come up with cryptic clues. It is easy to imagine that their creators might prefer to set themselves a more satisfying challenge than inauspiciously filling a thirteen-by-thirteen grid.

Having a hidden structure is also a good way to get started, rather than sitting there pondering the infinite possibilities of a blank grid like Buridan's ass in the fable, which finds itself stuck between two equally attractive piles of hay and, unable to rein in ambivalence and choose a favorite, dies of hunger.

There are assuredly many constructors for whom the basic unit of crosswording is the clue and not the grid, and who relish each clue as it comes. For others, filling a grid may raise the unanswerable question of where to start. If you know that you're going to try and construct a grid, though, whose perimeter reads TOBEORNOTTOBETHATISTHEQUESTION, well, you know what to do as you find yourself willingly thrown in at the deep end.

That's one reason for including a nina. Another is political. Take Hungary. Crosswords were banned there in 1925 when the Horthy government discovered that a monarchist constructor had hidden the message LONG LIVE OTTO in one of them. And when the final edition of the British tabloid *News of the World* was being prepared among the debris of the UK phone-hacking scandal, executive Rebekah Brooks may have had two senior colleagues comb the copy for messages from disgruntled staff, but they did not notice some seemingly pointed phrases in the clues within the quickie and the cryptic. Constructed, one suspects, less in sorrow than in anger, they included "woman stares wildly at calamity," "catastrophe," "stink," and "criminal enterprise."

Other "personal" ninas are happier and subtler: birthday wishes to loved ones, which, ultimately, have only one intended reader but which are so unrelated to the mechanics of solving the puzzle that those for whom they are not meant would be churlish in the extreme to resent their presence—much better to join in and relish the fun.

Among the most common ninas is a puzzle theme the constructor has decided not to announce—and you, the solver, only spot if you're letting your brain wander around. In 2009 Brendan Emmett Quigley constructed a puzzle for *The Guardian* in which the answers included PIERCE ("break through"), LINCOLN ("city"), GRANT ("admit"), HOOVER ("clean"), and FORD ("go to other bank"). It is easy to miss connections like this—especially if your obsession is the speed of your solve—but once you do, your heart is lifted, and there are extra treats, like the unchecked letters in the central column spelling out the by-then-inaugurated OBAMA.

Ninas work best when, like that example, they come in a place that feels right: in symmetrical form in the grid, as an acrostic in the clues, or—in a different context—in the same place in every paragraph. They can be a treat that reveals itself at the end, or can provide help with the meat-and-potatoes of the puzzle. Spotting a nina midsolve, perhaps in an inattentive moment, can make the endgame a lot smoother as you may be able rapidly to fill in more squares, and hence gain more letter clues to the actual clue clues.

Ninas are also a way for constructors to flex their muscles. Constructor Henry Hook showed his constructing chops at the age of fourteen. His grandmother gave him a puzzle that was part crossword, part jigsaw, created by Eugene T. Maleska, who went on to become the editor of the *New York Times* puzzle. Its endgame revealed a zigzagging nina reading, YOU HAVE JUST FINISHED THE WORLD'S MOST REMARKABLE CROSSWORD. Days after Hook received the gift, Maleska received a puzzle, written by Hook, with the nina WHAT MAKES YOU THINK YOUR PUZZLE IS MORE REMARKABLE THAN MINE? Most ninas, it has to be said, are considerably less bombastic, but many serve a similar purpose: to prove one's chops to one's peers. They also convey an extra aspect of the personality of the more playful constructor, raising spirits and making a personal connection with the solver, the pair drawn inalienably together in fun.

Such moments are all the more affecting when they take place in unlikely puzzles. The London *Times* has the most dependable of British crosswords: Constructors are anonymous to ensure a house style that does not allow for themes or even the inclusion of living persons with the exception of the reigning monarch. So when, in 1967, a teacher at Westcliff High School for Boys wrote to the paper to ask whether a relevant clue or answer might be included on the day of departure of Alfred Bately, the head of maths and an ardent *Times* solver, the answer was not unexpected. Written in a letter that seemed curt was the admonishment that "the crossword was certainly not the place for passing on personal messages!"

That seemed to be the end of it until the last day of the same term. Hidden in that day's apparently staid and anonymous puzzle were references including MATHEMATICS, GOODBYE MR. CHIPS, and even ALF, RED, BAT, and the cathedral city ELY. "It rapidly became clear to us," a colleague recalled, smitten in admiration, "that the crossword editor was not as stony-hearted as his letter had led us to believe."

Just as touching is the story of Wing Commander Peter Flippant, who entered the 1999 *Times* Crossword Championship. Eliminated at the first round, he offered his help as a companion-in-arms with the practical arrangements, in his words, "moving chairs and tables around and shuffling pieces of paper."

A couple of months later, the Saturday *Times* puzzle contained, with zero fanfare, the following laudation in answers placed consecutively in the grid: SQUADRON LEADER, PETER, FLIPPANT, THANKS.

The nina in its purest form, though, is probably the perimeter message of a puzzle by Monk for the *Financial Times* in 2007. It reads AGHBURZUMISHIKRIMPATUL, which is exactly the kind of gobbledygook that suggests that the solver has embarked on a wild-goose chase. AGHBURZUMISHIKRIMPATUL means nothing, even in a made-up language, surely?

Not so. It means something in the made-up language Black Speech, invented by J. R. R. Tolkien for the inhabitants of Mordor. In fact, it is inscribed on the golden, inaccessible One Ring in the *Lord of the Rings* trilogy:

Ash nazg durbatulûk, ash nazg gimbatul,
Ash nazg thrakatulûk agh burzum-ishi krimpatul.

And so our nina perimeter does mean something—"and in the darkness bind them"—monumentally irrelevant to the working of the puzzle as a crossword but a source of jaw-dropping joy and hats-off admiration to a tiny proportion of solvers. The nina, then, in a nutshell.

(While constructors might make their invisible messages so arcane that they are only spotted by a few, the puzzle itself is a different matter. For a solver—especially the more dogged [or perhaps I should use the obsolete term "caninal"?]—the feeling that he or she should have been able to fill the grid is assuredly no mere bonus . . .)

FAIR

Crossword constructors may play tricks but must also play fair

From the 1850s onward, Lewis Carroll devised a stream of puzzles for magazines. While they were ostensibly constructed for children, their linguistic and mathematical demands were beyond the capabilities of many of his adult readers. Had the crossword been born a half century earlier, it's no stretch to imagine Carroll as one of the greatest constructors in the game, probably appearing at the weekend with baroque themed challenges rather than in the weekday puzzles. His fictional characters show, to varying degrees, a keen grasp of what we would now call the constructor's art.

> *"Then you should say what you mean," the March Hare went on.*

"I do," Alice hastily replied; "at least—at least I mean what I say—that's the same thing, you know."

"Not the same thing a bit!" said the Hatter. "Why, you might just as well say that 'I see what I eat' is the same thing as 'I eat what I see'!"

Crossword constructors disagree on many things: the best balance of high- and lower-brow material, which words are old chestnuts, and whether one another's funny clues are, well, funny. But they all want to be seen to be fair.

The alternative—to be thought of as unsporting, recondite, or contemptuous toward the solver—is tantamount to being no fun, after all. And since the point of word games is to have fun, the unfair constructor will find that his or her career is as poor and short as it is nasty and brutish.

Editors of puzzle pages remind their charges of fairness when some constructor is trying to be too clever for the solver's own good—or simply rewrite the clues accordingly. The first creator of puzzles to express this desideratum in the form of an actual injunction was a British headmaster, Prebendary A. F. Ritchie, who took his pseudonym from the first five letters of his name, and also from a mischievous Arabic demon, Afrit.

Afrit's Injunction is given in the introduction to his 1949 collection *Armchair Crosswords*. "We must expect the composer to play tricks," insists Afrit, "but we shall insist that he play fair." After this, in bold:

You need not mean what you say, but you must say what you mean.

No decent constructor wants any of the clues in a puzzle to remain unsolved, but if you, the solver, are well and truly stumped, Afrit's Injunction means that, when you see the answer that defeated you, you should be able to look back at the clue and see that you could have solved it. Take this, from the London *Times*'s first constructor, Adrian Bell:

Die of cold?

Does Bell mean what he appears to be saying here? Of course not. A faithful paraphrase of the expression "die of cold" would be too mundane, not to mention morbid, for a diverting piece of entertainment. Once the solver has abandoned this image, considered other meanings of the word "die" and gone via "singular of dice" to the answer, ICECUBE, that is the moment of fun that is the point of the whole exercise.

Not only is it a relief to shift your brain from something as wretched as hypothermia to something as refreshing as an ice cube, there is also respect for the constructor. He didn't mean what he said, but he did say what he meant. All the information was there, presented in a form just misleading and unhelpful enough to be entertaining. Here's another of Bell's:

Spoils of War

Again, this clue does not mean what it says, and the answer is less dispiriting than looting in a combat zone: It's MARS. As Afrit says, a cryptic clue "may attempt to mislead by employing a form of words which can be taken in more than one way, and it is your fault if you take it the wrong way." Point taken.

So, the Mad Hatter would, like his creator Lewis Carroll, make a fine creator of crosswords:

> *"The question is," said Alice, "whether you can make words mean so many different things."*

Humpty Dumpty, on the other hand, would not:

> *"When I use a word," Humpty Dumpty said in rather a scornful tone, "it means just what I choose it to mean—neither more nor less."*

(And so for the constructor, the game can be fairly reinterpreted as: How much can I stretch language while still giving the solver a chance . . . ?)

WICKED

Words that aren't as helpful as they seem

In most crosswords, you know to be on your guard when solving a clue with a question mark at the end. The words that precede that question mark often have a natural feel. And the more conversational, the more apparently friendly a clue is, the greater the chance that the constructor means something very far from what he or she appears to be saying.

English is a language that abounds in ambiguity, and crosswording is a language that exploits this haziness. A few examples:

Words that end with ER: When you see the word "number," you naturally assume that it's doing the same job it always does: depicting ONE, say, or TEN, or even, as part of some wordplay, PI. But in the clue "Number of people in the theater?," you're looking for someone who does the numbing: an ANESTHESIOLOGIST. Likewise, a letter can be a landlady, a tower a horse, a sewer a seamstress—and a flower is so often a river in crosswords that seasoned solvers get tripped up when the word is actually used to mean a piece of flora.

Words that begin with DE: "Detailed," you tend to assume, means comprehensive, meticulous, blow-by-blow. But "Detailed by the farmer's wife?" equally fairly describes the THREEBLINDMICE. See also: "decrease" (iron), "delight" (extinguish), and "defile" (remove from the cabinet).

Words that are pronounced differently to how they appear: Outside of crosswords, something "wicked" is amoral, heinous, or abominable. But "Supporter of wicked things?" is, you have to admit, an accurate description of a CANDLESTICK. Try reading each of these aloud in your mind and see how they offer two options: "minute," "pate," "multiply," "wound," "drawer," "refuse," "sow," "console."

Misleading names: When you see the word "Nancy," your mind cycles through the options—from Sinatra to Pelosi, from Mitford to Drew. But "Nancy's breakfast?" is a way of saying "what they call breakfast in the French city Nancy," and so you might be expected to be thinking PETITDEJEUNER. Other words that may or may not be names—depending sometimes on the presence or otherwise of a capital—include "Job," "Pole," "Lent," "Mass," and of course "March," "May," and "August."

If you get tripped up by any of these, don't get frustrated: Think of it as a kind of friendly pun-ishment.

(And then there are those words that the seasoned solver comes to greet as longtime acquaintances . . .)

ALAMO

Words found more often in crosswords than in real life

Crossword English is a twisted version of the language. Do enough puzzles and you'll soon become more familiar with the Italian river the PO and the Sumerian city-state UR than you would ever otherwise have been. In the trade, they're called crosswordese.

Such words occur more regularly in crosswords than they do in, say, conversation. Some are good at making up parts of other, longer expressions; others fit conveniently into a grid when you need, say, a four-letter word with a vowel at each end, like ASEA, made entirely of very common English-language letters.

Most solvers develop a feel for such words, but web developer and data journalist Noah Veltman went one further and got some figures and lists. Through solving, he had become attached to words such as OLEO and OLIO and started to take an interest in their regular appearance. He took a database of the clues and answers in the *New York Times* crossword from 1996 to 2012 and compared the frequency with which words appear there with how often they crop up in the same period, but in another context: Google's database of twenty million books.

One word that doesn't appear in any of those twenty million books is "crosswordiness," Veltman's splendid term to denote a word's quality of appearing more often in a crossword than in real life—or, at least, one measure of real life.

The constellations with names beginning URSA, the Texan mission the ALAMO, the name NOEL, the spirit ARIEL, the copy editor's instruction STET, and the ardent desires known as YENS are among those words that score highest. All of them, when judiciously placed in a grid, increase the number of possible words for the entries that cross with them because of the presence of vowels and other oft-seen letters, or of those letters that, like Y, are often found at the end of a word. This also explains why, as crossword constructor, editor, and teacher Don Manley puts it in his *Chambers Crossword Manual*, you can "expect to find ELEMENT and EVEREST frequently, especially along the edge," offering a bounty of those Es with which so many other words end.

Part of the job of a crossword editor is to make sure that the "crosswordiest" words don't become tiresome—and kudos to all the editors for this ongoing fight. But don't be mistaken: Shunning cliché is not the same as making crossword language the same as our everyday lexicon. Manley continues by asking the solver to forgive the constructors their fillers.

"Learn to regard them," he advises, "as old friends." Indeed, many solvers enjoy the discovery of new words through puzzles, and for any familiar entry there will always be a constructor with a fresh way of cluing it. Georges Perec, the French constructor and experimental author, describes well this ever-increasing pressure on the makers of crosswords. In his splendidly titled book *Les Mots croisés, procédés de considérations de l'auteur sur l'art et la manière de croiser les mots*, he insists that the greatest call on a constructor's ingenuity is made by the shortest words, those "which hold the grid together." In French, the old chestnuts include IO, ANA, ENEE, and UTE, all of which would be equally helpful for English-language constructors.

"The constructor makes it a point of honor," remarks Perec, "to find for each of these a clue that no-one has used before."

Here's to that honor, and here are ten of the English language's most crosswordy words, the unusually shaped faithful friends to constructors, and ones you meet sooner or later in Crosswordland.

ALEE: The lee side of a vessel is the one that's sheltered from the wind. ALEE can be an adverb meaning "away from the wind" or an order to put the helm toward the lee. It goes back at least as far as the fourteenth century and, as even the most casual fan of medieval alliterative debate poetry can tell you, is to be found in the anonymous poem "Mum and the Sothsegger."

ARGO: Reimmortalized in *Jason and the Argonauts*, famous for Ray Harryhausen's ingenious stop-motion effects, these Greek heroes sailed on the ARGO in search of the Golden Fleece. The entry has also been clued as "Cornstarch brand" after the sauce thickener that may have cannily coined its name so as to appear near the top of alphabetical product lists, but the 2012 Oscars' Best Picture provides a more contemporary alternative.

ASEA: Hyphenated in the Oxford dictionary and defined as "On the sea, at sea; to the sea," ASEA also lends itself to misleading definitions via the names of the various bodies of waters, such as in Eugene T. Maleska's pert clue "In the Black?"

EMU: Words that start and end with a vowel are always useful, and sometimes those vowels just have to be E and U. Alternatives do exist: EAU is used in English as a fancy way of saying "water," and the European Monetary System once experimented with the ECU as a kind of single currency. But the plump, flightless Australasian bird is the go-to entry when you just have to end a three-letter word with a U. The less frequent appearance of the EMU in crosswords was mourned repeatedly by P. G. Wodehouse (see the chapter PLUM below).

ERATO: The inspiration—if you happen to be an ancient Greek—for lyric love poetry, and far more beloved of crossword constructors than her sister Muses MEL-

POMENE, TERPSICHORE, or POLYHYMNIA. A favorite ruse of cryptic constructors is to make "muse" appear to be working as the verb meaning "to reflect or to gaze ponderously" when it should be read as a noun, thereby disguising the reference to this desirable five-letter string.

IAMBI: In the Greek, whence it comes, a lampoon, because of the tradition in satirical verse of following a short beat with a long. "The woods decay, the woods decay and fall," wrote Tennyson in the da-dum da-dum form known as iambic pentameter. "Iambus" is the singular term if you're into analyzing the basic units of poetic rhythm, and two or more of these "feet" are IAMBI. Can also be clued rudely, as with Monk's "Feet using which I can go either way?"

PSST: If you count Y as a vowel in all but name, there are vanishingly few four-consonant words. CWMS, the plural of a Welsh valley, doesn't really count since W is standing in as a vowel, as anyone who's passed a sign reading SNWKER HALL in Cefn y Dyniewyd can testify. TBSP, TSPS, and other terms you might find in recipe books are, of course, available, but if you eschew abbreviations, you're pretty much left with two interjections: BRRR and PSST.

SMEE: The second-most crosswordy word in Noah Veltman's analysis, SMEE has changed its role as an answer. Once teasingly depicted in a *Punch* cartoon in which one duck tells another that she is a SMEE, "only found in crosswords," the avian type—which may also be a smew, a pochard, a wigeon, or a wagtail—has given way to the pirate who, we are told in *Peter Pan*, "stabbed without offense," as in John Lampkin's *Los Angeles Times* clue "Barrie baddie."

SOHO: Or, as it is often rendered, "SoHo," for the Lower Manhattan neighborhood that's SOuth of HOuston Street. Its equivalent in London, the boho Soho, is on a site once used for hunting, and named after an Anglo-Norman phrase hollered by huntsmen: "Soho!," most likely an expression of purely exclamatory origin. SOHO can be also rendered with a hyphen, as in *The Two Gentlemen of Verona* ("Run, boy, run, run, and seek him out. / So-ho! so-ho!") and all in capitals for those who work remotely in a "Small Office Home Office."

STYE: Edward Moor's 1823 *Suffolk Words and Phrases: or, An Attempt to Collect the Lingual Localisms of That County* defines this word as "a troublesome little excrescence or pimple on the eye-lid" and prescribes the application of a gold ring; today, the preferred treatment is a warm compress and some painkillers.

(The crossword is a kind of love letter to the English language. And as we shall see, the affection is mutual . . .)

AUTHORSHIP

Why English-language crosswords bear the names of their constructors

Like many American inventions, the crossword became, in the twentieth century, a global phenomenon. Browse at newspaper kiosks and bookshops around the world, and you'll see Greek, Persian, Japanese, and Tamil surrounding those familiar-looking grids. However, the crossword is not ubiquitous—some languages do not take kindly to being broken into pieces and plotted in interlocking squares.

Where it does appear, the culture of crosswords adapts to its environment. Some differences are visual: In South American puzzles, the clues live in the grid, printed in tiny type with arrows indicating the direction of the answers; the squares of the smaller Japanese grids each take one syllable rather than one letter.

More important—and something for its speakers to celebrate—is the greater scope afforded to constructors who work in English. English may be called a Germanic language, but it's more like a mélange, salmagundi, or omnium-gatherum: For any English word with a German origin, there may well be a perfectly usable alternative brought to Britain by the Norman French or something with a Latin flavor.

And so, as the Oxford Dictionaries website carefully words it, "it seems quite probable that English has more words than most comparable world languages." There are many different ways of denoting the same objects and actions, but all are valid parts of the English lexicon. If you want to hint at some word or other, your options may well be multiple—even the definitions under that word in a dictionary will offer alternatives of varying degrees of delight. No wonder the English language is well suited to the crossword.

When the crossword was on the rise, London *Times* editor George Geoffrey Dawson wondered if there were any better reason for the existence of words such as CADI, EFFENDI, MUEZZIN, and VIZIER than "to get crossword composers out of trouble." It's as if Dawson had tried to construct a puzzle himself, got frustrated when he found he'd constructed himself into a corner that needed a very un-English-looking word, and then realized that some exotic term imported from Turkey might just do the job.

It's certainly true that English has always been happy to absorb words from places with which Britain has traded or that have been part of its empire, thus further expanding the vocabulary available to the creators of word games.

The existence of multiple words for any one given thing makes English not especially friendly toward nonnative speakers trying to learn the language, but on the upside, it's perfect for games that involve words, terms, designations, expressions, and utterances.

The obverse is also true: The existence of so many words with multiple meanings is a boon to constructors. Want to write a misleading clue where a perfectly ordinary word turns out to signify something quite unexpected? English is your language.

All those choices mean that the crossword constructor is no mere paraphraser. Each time she chooses one interpretation of a word over another, or a circuitous route in preference to a direct one, she is expressing her personality. And so it is little surprise that solvers can have favorite constructors and develop over years of grid filling a sense that they know their favorites—that they understand how those challenging minds work. Can you say the same of the creators of other puzzles like word searches or sudokus?

In non-English-language puzzles, named constructors are rare and the crossword sits on the puzzle page, impersonal and apparently aloof. They have their own pleasures—the cheery, inclusive way that È, É, and Ê are all rendered E in the French puzzle, for example—but the clueing cannot compete. And why put your name to a list of synonyms? English-language constructors, having all those extra words to play with, are, in contrast, regarded more like authors. And rightly so.

(And so any puzzle, in whatever language, should be approached by the nonnative speaker with extreme caution. After all, it's not like you can just translate a clue from one language to another. Can you . . . ?)

TRANSLATION

How on earth do you translate a crossword puzzle?

You might wonder why anyone would ever translate a crossword clue, but some people have to. Take the scene in *The West Wing* where President Jed Bartlet calls out a clue to the First Lady: "It may be bitter (3)." He considers TEA, makes a wisecrack that WOMAN doesn't fit, and his wife, Abbey, rebukes him: "END, you idiot, bitter END."

In the DVD's French subtitles, this becomes "*Peut être amer*," with a letter count of three. This is fine for THÉ, the French for tea, and FEMME still doesn't fit, but the translator has Abbey offer RIRE as the correct answer. It's a plausible answer—"*rire amer*" meaning "bitter laugh"—except that it's too long. Faced with the challenge of finding two same-length words that might fit (or even making it a four-letter answer and having

Jed say "THÉ is too short, but FEMME is too long"), the translation runs away and hides.

The Swedish and Norwegian subtitles are even more cowardly, removing Abbey's line altogether. It's a shame, since the words are not random: The important ones are END (foreshadowing Abbey's agonizing investigation for medical misconduct) and WOMAN (because Jed has been impatient with Abbey's indecision over earrings). TEA is the least important word in the exchange and certainly isn't the one to base the translation's letter count on.

And if that seems like an involved process for a throwaway gag at the top of an episode of a TV program, consider the challenge of translating something larger. What if the material in a fictional crossword was more important? What if wordplay was part of the original text?

In Georges Perec's French-language novel *La Vie mode d'emploi*, we find an unfinished puzzle in the room of one of the characters reproduced in the text. The rest of the book is riddled with cross-references, puns, and hidden expressions, so the task facing the translator is daunting: How do you re-create a collection of words, preserving not only their meaning but also the characteristics that allow them to intersect with one another in a grid? And since a seasoned solver might look at the grid and wonder which words might fit the empty spaces, should the gaps be taken into consideration, too?

Happily, Perec was aware of this potential problem and furnished his German translator Eugen Helmlé with notes about the novel's wordplay. In the case of the crossword, his instructions were that only ETONNEMENT and OIGNON

E	T	O	N	N	E	M	E	N	T
P	R	I	S	O	N	N	I	E	R
R	A	G	■	I		■			
O	I	N	D	R	E	■			
U	T	O	■	C			■		
V	E	N		I				■	
E	M	■		R					
T	E			■			■		
T	N	■			■				
E	T								

A	S	T	O	N	I	S	H	E	D
P	O	■	N				■		
A	L		I				■		
R	I	S	O	T	T	O			
T	L		N	■	■				
M	O								
E	Q								
N	U						■		
T	Y	■					■		
S	S	N	O	R	M	A	N	D	Y

mattered. And so, in David Bellos's English translation, we see ASTONISHED and ONION among other unrelated words. Bellos told me that the inclusion of a potential TLON in his version of this fictional puzzle is a nod to the imaginary world in the title of Jorge Luis Borges's "Tlön, Uqbar, Orbis Tertius," which seems a suitably *perécienne* flourish.

He added a regret about his translation of the grid: The placement of ONION means that there's an impossible entry ending with O in the English version of the grid. So if you have a copy of Perec's *Life: A User's Manual*, you should pull out a pencil and add an extra black square to the grid, in this case in the space immediately following ONION.

And if you're an experimental novelist with, for whatever reason, a grudge against translators, you might consider creating a book featuring a puzzle in which the clues, the entries, and the way they intersect are vital to the plot. A translation of the grid would be likely to necessitate a different grid, and vice versa. As Bellos remarked, "It would be a paradoxical and fuse-blowing project."

(In the interests of sanity, then, let's stick to our native tongue. Ah, but if only it were that simple. Are we talking about English as she was written in poetry and prose, where every word has a long and distinguished history, or as she is spoken, where new words appear as if from nowhere . . . ?)

UNABLE TO USE JARGON?

CANT

The irresistible rise of slang

Stanley Newman now holds a respectable role as *Newsday*'s puzzle editor, but in the 1980s, he was an enfant terrible of the crosswording world—or, as he terms it, one of the New Wave. He lay down his equivalent of Luther's Ninety-five Theses in his Crossworder's Own Newsletter, taking potshots at the then puzzle editor of *The New York Times*, Eugene T. Maleska, for running crosswords best suited to "the residents of a retirement home for university dons."

Newman believed that there was a younger audience for crosswords—one that was more comfortable with modern colloquialisms and pop culture than with arcane geographical and historical references.

Maleska appeared unconcerned, referring to the New Wave as "the Newman ripple" and to Newman himself as "that pipsqueak." But the New Wavers won the war: After Maleska's death in 1993, the *New York Times*'s puzzle developed, under its new editor, Will Shortz, into a form not at all dissimilar to that envisaged by Newman and his votaries.

It was the same in Britain. At Christmas 1966, *The Guardian* held a competition in which readers were invited to send in crosswords. The winner was David Moseley. He received six guineas and an invitation to submit more puzzles—which he now has been doing, as Gordius, for nearly half a century. However, amid the praise for his 1966 winning entry, there was a caveat from the puzzle editor John Perkin: "There are one or two things that I wouldn't normally let through. 'Booze' is slang and you use it twice."

Nowadays, any crossword editor would still judge that any crossword with the same word twice is a less satisfying solve, but BOOZE would pass without comment. In the sixties, though, the crossword was younger and anxious to appear respectable. University slang such as DON was acceptable, but BOOZE? A little too rowdy.

Happily, some words have almost disappeared from puzzles. Midwestern towns, population in three figures, the names of which their near neighbors would struggle to recall? Much less often spied in puzzles. And the little Latin words that completed arcane quotations and reassured newspaper readers that solving was not an activity to feel ashamed of? Almost entirely eradicated.

Something had to take their place: something with unusual spellings and plenty of nice wee short words. That something was the irrepressibly fertile font of slang. So just as Arthur

Wynne's first crossword had "A river in Russia" to clue NEVA, so in 2008 did Brendan Emmett Quigley clue the same four letters with "'— Get Enuf' (3LW song)," exploiting the voguish penchant for misspelling among R&B songwriters.

It happens, though, that slang is more likely to flourish in environments where speakers aren't keen on outsiders being able to fully understand them. Teenagers resentful of their parents are one such group—and so are thieves, vagabonds, and users of narcotics, all of whose language makes the crossword a saltier place than it was in the days of Maleska and the young Gordius. After all, anyone who is trying to hide what he or she is really trying to say is engaged in the same activity as a devious crossword constructor.

Take cocaine. Present-day solvers aren't expected to be frequent users of addictive alkaloids, (notwithstanding the English humorist Stephen Fry's former habit of taking the drug before tackling the hardest British crosswords). They would, though, do well to acquaint themselves with its nicknames: ICE, C, COKE, CANDY, READYWASH, CHARLIE, and BLOW, as listed in *The Chambers Dictionary*. And a constructor might induce you to take a hit of a heroin synonym such as HORSE, H, JUNK, SNOW, and SUGAR. And what can beat "drug" to indicate the most common vowel in English? You could almost suspect that ecstasy was given its shortest nickname by constructors bored of using "east" (E on a compass), "Spain" (E on the back of a car), and "base" (2.71828, or *e* in mathematical formulas).

That isn't to say that slang now habitually passes without notice. On January 7, 2012, *The New York Times* used the clue

"Wack, as in hip hop" for ILLIN. Word soon reached the national press that a solver had complained that "wack" has a negative sense, and that ILLIN is its opposite. The tone of the coverage was generally derisive and seemed based on an assumption that the crossword was still a fusty corner of culture.

How, pundits wondered, could those tweedy crossword-constructor types expect that experimenting with hip-hop terminology could result in anything other than embarrassment?

Crosswords are slightly older (when the clue was published, ninety-eight years old) than B-boying (around forty years old), but there's a good reason why puzzlers might take an active interest in hip-hop: Both activities promote flipping the meanings of words. Hence, in crosswords, clues such as "To show or not to show?," which exploits two meanings of SCREEN, and "Chopstick?" for CLEAVE. In crosswords and in hip-hop, this ambiguity is quite deliberate (that's "quite" as in "completely," not as in "to a limited extent").

As Run-DMC helpfully pointed out in their track "Peter Piper," the big bad wolf in your neighborhood, rather than being "bad" meaning "bad" might in fact be "bad" meaning "good." See also WICKED, especially if it comes from a Bostonian—though F. Scott Fitzgerald did have a character use that word in a positive sense in 1920.

And so it is with ILL. In 1979, the Sugarhill Gang used it in a negative sense, contrasting an urge to act civilized with the temptation to "act real ill." But by 1986, when the Beastie Boys proclaimed themselves the "most illin-est" B-boys, that was a boast.

So even if WACK flipped its meaning, too, the clue is sound

either way. That is to say, it's not bad. Before sanctioning a crossword editor for a lack of oversight, consider whether the clue really deserves a cool response. You might think better of it.

(The cultural changes between NEVA's being clued as a Russian river and with an allusion to "Neva Get Enuf" are echoed in a pleasing pair of anagrams. Back in the day, constructors noted with delight that PRESBYTERIAN was an apposite anagram of "best in prayers." More recently, many have spotted that it's just as pleasing a jumble of "Britney Spears." Welcome to the modern world . . .)

THE LATEST, FROM ALL CORNERS OF THE GLOBE?

NEWS

How the news can dribble into the puzzle

Very often, the crossword becomes news. One morning at the Scott Lithgow shipyard in Scotland in 1981, two welders were tackling the *Financial Times* crossword while they waited for a welding rod to be repaired; a manager told them to put away the puzzle, and when they refused, both were suspended. Following a disciplinary hearing during which they apologized, one was further suspended and the other sacked, and their fellow shipbuilders went on strike in solidarity.

This local incident was reported in the national press, and it wasn't pegged as an industrial-relations report. The tone was one of incredulity. Welders tackling a cryptic crossword? And in the posh people's *Financial Times*, at that? In the 1980s the perception of a class divide was still very strong: Quick crosswords in tabloids were for the workers; cryptics were for those who had had a classical education.

And sometimes, the travel is in the other direction: from the news part of the newspaper into the puzzle. Happily, this is seldom. The puzzle provides a haven for anyone who has bought a newspaper and then realized that there is something unbearable about current affairs and a comfort of abstraction in the sturdy reliable grid.

This is put most succinctly by Joan Didion in her study of bereavement, *The Year of Magical Thinking*, when she describes going straight from the front page of *The New York Times* to the puzzle page:

> *. . . a way of starting the day that had become during those months a pattern, the way I had come to read, or more to the point not to read, the paper.*

The flip side is that when the puzzle does reflect what's going on among the other pages, the effect can be magical in a different sense. The greatest example is best told in reverse chronological order.

January 2004, Butler University, Indiana: Mathematics professor Jerry Farrell takes part in an online interview. After discussing a puzzle he wrote in 1996, he shares with his interviewer a special "telekinesis puzzle" he has since constructed. The solver begins by tossing a coin. Heads or tails?

November 6, 1996, a newspaper kiosk in New York City: The lead story in the newspaper is CLINTON ELECTED.

November 5, 1996, the office of the *New York Times* puzzle editor: The phone rings. It is a crossword solver, angry that puzzle editor Will Shortz has been using the *New York Times* crossword to promote his personal political views. It rings again. Another solver is infuriated by Shortz's presumption in predicting the outcome of the fifty-third presidential election. It is polling day and the votes have not yet all been cast, let alone counted. The phone continues to ring . . .

Earlier that morning, in the home of a *New York Times* solver: Outside, people are heading to the polling stations to cast a vote for Bob Dole or Bill Clinton (or, indeed for Ross Perot or Ralph Nader). Inside, the solver looks at the day's puzzle in *The New York Times*. She fills the third row from the top with the answer to 17 across's "Forecast"—PROGNOSTICATION—and then the third row from the bottom with MISTERPRESIDENT, which directs her to the middle row. This row has two clues, both of them unusual:

39A. Lead story in tomorrow's newspaper (!), with 43A
43A. See 39A

Forty-three across is clear from the crossing letters: ELECTED. The solver frowns. Tomorrow's newspaper will of course lead on the victory of whoever is elected, but there's no way that headline, with the name of the victor, can be an entry in today's puzzle. Surely that's not the PROGNOSTICATION?

It is. The down clues that cross with 39 across spell it out: CAT ("Black Halloween animal"), LUI ("French 101 word"), IRA ("Provider of support, for short"), YARN ("Sewing shop purchase"), BITS ("Short writings"), BOAST ("Trumpet"), and NRA ("Much-debated political inits."). The middle row reads: CLINTONELECTED. The solver picks up the telephone.

Earlier that morning, in the home of another *New York Times* solver: Another solver frowns at the grid. "Lead story in tomorrow's newspaper?" He fills in the squares of 39 across with help from the down clues: BAT ("Black Halloween animal"), OUI ("French 101 word"), BRA ("Provider of support, for short"), YARD ("Sewing shop purchase"), BIOS ("Short writings"), BLAST ("Trumpet"), and ERA ("Much-debated political inits."). The middle row reads: BOBDOLE-ELECTED. The solver picks up the telephone.

Earlier that year: The candidates in the forthcoming election are confirmed as Bob Dole and Bill Clinton (and Ross Perot and Ralph Nader). A math professor and occasional puzzle constructor named Jerry Farrell asks *New York Times* puzzle editor Will Shortz if he remembers the puzzle that Farrell submitted to the paper in 1980. Shortz does.

1980, the offices of *Games* magazine: *Games* editor Will Shortz receives a crossword puzzle that has been rejected by *The New York Times*. He thinks it is "pretty amazing" but can't accept it as it is beyond the deadline for the November/December issue and the puzzle needs to be published before Election Day on November 4.

Earlier that year, the office of the *New York Times* puzzle editor: *New York Times* puzzle editor Eugene T. Maleska receives a puzzle from math professor and occasional puzzle constructor Jerry Farrell in which the entries that intersect with 1 across are devised such that the first answer in the grid can equally validly take CARTER or REAGAN, clued as the winner of the forthcoming election. He rejects the puzzle, asking, "What if Anderson wins?" Maleska has been in the post for three years but already has a reputation for fastidiousness and fustiness. It is unclear whether his rejection is motivated by a conviction that independent candidate John B. Anderson might break the two-party stranglehold on American politics, by a sense of loyalty to another man who uses a middle initial, or by a sense that *The New York Times* is not in the business of provoking solvers and messing with political crystal balls . . . and never will be.

So much for continuity. Here, in the same spirit, is Jerry Farrell's telekinesis puzzle (answers in the Resources section at the end of the book):

The solver begins by tossing a coin and writing HEAD or TAIL as 1 across in a four-by-three grid.

Across	**Down**
1 Your coin shows a _____	*1 Half a laugh*
5 Wagner's earth goddess	*2 Station terminus?*
6 Word with one or green	*3 Dec follower?*
4 Certain male →	

1	2	3	4
5			
6			

Postscript: On July 9, 2003, a *New York Times* puzzle by Patrick Merrell had at 20 across TOURDEFRANCE and at 35 across "[Prediction] Lance Armstrong at the end of the 2003 20-Across": Both FOURTIME-CHAMP and FIVETIMECHAMP were valid entries, and the first letters of the first seven clues spelled out F-A-R-R-E-L-L, an appropriately arcane accolade.

(The CLINTON/BOBDOLE puzzle is treasured by American solvers. Its equivalent in the UK is a puzzle that contains the clue “Poetical scene with surprisingly chaste Lord Archer vegetating [3, 3, 8, 12].” If that means nothing to you, you are not alone. It is time to take a peek at the British cryptic and its celebration of sometimes baffling wordplay. Let’s start with an example of the British love of mucking about with language . . .)

SPOONER

The Brit who is treasured for the way he mangled language

A child might look twice at the title of Shel Silverstein's story *Runny Babbit* and ask, with some justification, what a "babbit" is. But by the subtitle, *A Billy Sook*, all is clear. Without much direction, the reader twigs that reading this silly book will involve switching the sounds at the beginnings of pairs of words.

So it is in crosswords: Take Patrick Berry's 2011 puzzle in which "handle with care" becomes CANDLEWITHHAIR and "letterbox" BETTERLOCKS. And in British crosswords, that delight in nonsense goes at least double.

If the clues in a British crossword appear to be the kind of gobbledygook from which only a masochist could derive the slightest pleasure, it might help to bear in mind that Britain is a place that has made a heroic institution of an otherwise little-known cleric for a kind of speech impediment.

That cleric was the Reverend William Archibald Spooner—indeed, Berry's puzzle is a little fantasia in which we imagine Rev. Spooner as a new employee of the USPS—but he was not the first to mangle words in this distinctive manner.

In his 1865 dictionary of slang, John Hotten writes about a "disagreeable nonsense" then in vogue among medical students at London University.

The waggish undergraduate habit of referring to a mutton chop as a "chutton mop" and a pint of stout as a "stint of pout" was named "the Gower Street dialect" after the university's location; before this, such mangled phrases were known as "marrowskies," apparently after a violin-playing Polish count who was two and a half feet tall and amused upper-class women with the same kind of wordplay. However, in 1879, as soon as Dr. Spooner introduced a hymn as "Kinqering kongs their titles take," his fate was sealed. His students began to refer to him as "the Spoo" and awaited his every gaffe with gusto.

It was a long wait: In fact, Dr. Spooner did not perpetrate many eponymous isms. His biographers and students of language have been unable to verify "The Lord is a shoving leopard," "Three cheers for the queer old dean," or "The half-warmed fish in your hearts." "You have hissed all my mystery lectures, tasted the whole worm, and must leave by the next town drain"? Far, far too good to be true. Even some of the slips of the tongue that are reliably reported have been tidied up for greater effect: His announcement that a bride and groom had been "loifully jawned in holy matrimony" became in legend the more powerful "jawfully loined." The current edition of *The Oxford Dictionary of Quotations* is happy only with the disappointing "weight of rages." As the 1928 *New York Times* headline put it, SPOONERISMS WERE FAKED—OXFORD DEAN'S ALLEGED LINGUAL SLIPS INVENTED BY STUDENTS.

So it's tricky not to pity the Spoo. Already an awkward enough fellow that he absentmindedly poured claret onto a pile of spilled salt (that one does have a reliable witness), he was unable to deliver a lecture on Tacitus or William of Wykeham without feeling that the undergraduates were hoping he might twist a phrase or two to rude or amusing effect. The rambunctious Maurice Bowra recalled in his memoirs:

> *Once after a bump-supper we serenaded him and stood outside his window calling for a speech. He put his head out and said, "You don't want a speech. You only want me to say one of those things," and immediately withdrew.*

In 1912 Spooner visited South Africa and wrote home to his wife: "The Johannesburg paper had an article on my visit to Johannesburg, but of course they thought me most famous for my Spoonerisms, so I was not greatly puffed up."

So why is it now the spoonerism rather than the gowerism or the marrowsky? One difference is that the medical students and the count were deliberately playing games with language, while Spooner's isms were, in myth and in reality, accidental. Unintended slips of the tongue are funny in a different way, suggesting a cheering, if fanciful, way of looking at the man. If Dr. Spooner is not to be remembered for his scholarship or his guardianship of New College, then, rather than as an embarrassment, we should think of him as the embodiment of the unconscious bleeding out into the social—a subversive figure who reveals what can happen when language breaks down.

It is not just the Brits who are taken with spoonerisms; a more intellectual approach is taken by the French with what they call the *contrepet*. The early French surrealists deliberately switched syllables in their prose to attack the idea that words and sentences have fixed meanings. Marcel Duchamp's "*Esquivons les ecchymoses des Esquimaux aux mots exquis*" has a surface meaning of sorts ("Let's dodge the bruising of Eskimos with exquisite words"), but its real intent is to force the reader to make fleeting connections that would otherwise seem irrational between Eskimos and language, language and the body, the body and Eskimos . . . and so on. Once you unshackle sounds from their apparent meaning, your mind is better able to question the so-called order of the world around you, which, in the experience of the surrealists, had just proved its own nonsensicality in four years of world war. Being French, they also found wordplay *très amusant*.

The descendants of the surrealists, the experimental writers of Oulipo (the Ouvroir de Littérature Potentielle, or Workshop of Potential Literature), were equally fond of the device. Luc Étienne's book *The Art of the Spoonerism*, recalled that, during the Occupation, Parisians "took a special pleasure in seeing under Métropolitain in their sad underground stations the sacrilegious inscription '*Pétain mollit trop*'"—"Pétain is getting too soft." For Étienne, this is as good an example as any of the subversive potential of the spoonerism: "a weapon of freedom."

The memoirs of Resistance secret agent Colonel Rémy take a similar joy in recalling how he arranged for the "prudish" BBC to broadcast French-language radio messages across the Channel, unaware that they contained scurrilous spoonerisms to cheer up the occupied, such as "*Duce, tes gladiateurs circulent dans le sang!*" The Beeb "would have shuddered at the mere thought of its airwaves being used to disseminate such imagery." It's safe to say that, in the 1940s, the BBC had never broadcast anything quite as rude. I would advise the sensitive francophone reader to skip to the next paragraph; for the rest of you, the phrase can be translated as "Mussolini, your gladiators are bloodstained," but also despoonerized to "*Duce, tes gladiateurs s'enculent dans le cirque*" ("your gladiators fuck one another in the circus"), a salty allusion to the decadent days of Rome.

In linguistics, too, the spoonerism is more than a passing slip of the tongue. Even though they're emitted in error, reported spoonerisms share many characteristics; they even seem to have a structure. The affected words are always close together, and one of the affected syllables is the one that would be stressed in the correct version of the utterance. More often than not, the swap involves an adjective and a noun; more often than by chance, the spoonerized phrase consists of two real words, however nonsensical they are in context. And when the spoonerized words are not real words, they usually sound as if they could be.

Crossword fans are used to the experience of being baffled by a clue but knowing some of the letters in an answer thanks to those that cross with it. If you think that the answer is a word you haven't heard before, it's a question of making up words in your head that fit. You concoct something plausibly pronounceable that sounds like other words—which seems to be the kind of thing that's taking place at great speed in spoonerisms. A spoonerized phrase might lack literal meaning, but it's never rhythmically clumsy: There's poetry in the poppycock. You might find that you've said the phrase "a picky truzzle" but not "a wosscrurd": Even your errors are made up of words that are real, or could be in your language.

That's why the best-loved spoonerisms are those that work just as well as the intended phrase, and why the spoonerism lives on in humor and in puzzles. The long-running British sketch show *The Two Ronnies* repeatedly exploited its scurrilous potential, producing lines such as "The rutting season for tea cozies" and "You're much too titty to be a preacher," just as Dr. Spooner's students did two generations earlier.

In the crossword century, constructors were not slow to pick up on the potential for puzzles in spoonerisms, and solvers are nowadays asked to come up with spoonerized phrases and reverse engineer the answer. One of the creators of the cryptic crossword, the poet and translator Edward Powys Mathers, gave a section in his 1934 collection *The Torquemada Puzzle Book* to challenges of the type: "When spoonerized, what aid to illumination suggests a slim sorceress?" (LIGHTSWITCH via "slight witch").

The puzzle magazine *The Enigma* used to run a form of puzzle that it called a spoonergram, where you replace the capitalized words in a piece of (slightly dodgy) verse with two phrases, one of which is a spoonerism of the other:

(4 5; 4 5)
His pretty love was young, petite.
Her FIRST adorned by silken bow;
They shared Sauternes, their joy complete;
Their kisses had a LAST, you know.

That's TINYWAIST and WINYTASTE. Nowadays, a devoted solver of British cryptics expects to find about one spoonerism a week, tackling clues like:

An insect to flit past, according to Spooner (9)
Spooner's "you're such a gorgeous pipistrelle"—no charge? (4, 7)

The answers are BUTTERFLY (via "flutter by," by Don Manley) and FLATBATTERY (via "bat flattery," by Paul). And the same kind of thing comes up in American puzzles: *The New York Times* has offered "Old comic actor's Little Bighorn headline?," "Controls a prison guard like a pop singer?," and "Writer-turned-Utah carpenter?," for BUSTERKEATON ("Custer beaten"), JAMESTAYLOR ("tames jailer") and NORMANMAILER ("Mormon nailer").

Such American spoonerisms cannot be filed merely under oddities or gags: The spoonerism played an important part in the humans-versus-machines battle at the 1999 American Crossword Puzzle Tournament. That year, spoonerisms such as "May I sew you to a sheet" (another one attributed to Dr. Spooner) were the reason that a nonhuman entrant, the computer program Proverb, slipped down the rankings—spoonerisms made a lot more sense to flesh-and-blood contestants, a difference we will return to later in the book.

(So if the American puzzle may include the occasional spoonerism or cryptic definition, the British crossword is perhaps best understood as a form where that kind of wordplay takes place, unflagged, in every clue. Tempted? You are in good company . . .)

SONDHEIM

Stephen Sondheim, British crosswording ambassador

During the writing of *West Side Story* in the midfifties, there was a predictable weekly drop in the productivity of lyricist Stephen Sondheim and composer Leonard Bernstein.

Sondheim had a habit of picking up a copy of a British weekly magazine called *The Listener* every Thursday on his way to meet his colleague. He bought it for the crossword. "I got Leonard Bernstein hooked," he remembered. "Thursday afternoons, no work got done on *West Side Story*. We were doing the puzzle."

The pair would also race each other to do anagrams—and the winner was always the lyricist, a man so enamored of wordplay that, one biographer claims, he submitted a crossword puzzle to *The New York Times* at the age of fourteen. Sadly for the crossover between musical theater and wordplay, the puzzle was unpublished and no copy is known to exist now.

The injustice was rectified in 1968, when *New York* magazine published a series of cryptic puzzles constructed by Sondheim. He introduced the first with an essay provocatively titled "How to Do a Real Crossword Puzzle, Or What's a Four-letter Word for 'East Indian Betel Nut' and Who Cares?"

Sondheim makes the case that cryptic crosswords are more satisfying than those with a higher proportion of definitional clues, writing fondly of the cryptic's demand that the solver follow the train of thought of a "devious mind," invidiously compared to the encyclopedic memory demanded by regular puzzles. Sondheim grants that the conventions of the British puzzle take a little getting used to; all it takes, he reassures, "is inexhaustible patience."

And then there are his puzzles, modeled on those he and Bernstein had enjoyed so much in *The Listener*. These are as enjoyable examples as any of the eye-wateringly arcane "advanced cryptic."

Arcane? Advanced? Indeed. *The Listener* was a magazine founded by the BBC in 1929: No mere listings rag, it had the mission of providing easy access to highbrow, often modernist, ideas. Contributors were to include Virginia Woolf, T. S. Eliot, and an eighteen-year-old Philip Larkin.

Its first puzzle appeared on April 2, 1930, offering as a prize "an invitation to visit the B.B.C. Studios on certain afternoons." Only one correct solution was received, from a Mr. I. Cresswell of Colchester; some later puzzles would receive none. But it is much loved: The puzzle moved to the London *Times* when *The*

Listener folded in 1991; six years later, when *The Times* wondered about devoting valuable space to a relatively niche feature, its future was discussed in Parliament and, happily, the strange crossword survives into the millennium.

Not only is its language abstruse—solvers are recommended to have at hand a copy of the capacious *Chambers Dictionary*, which contains many words once used by some poet or other and since forgotten—but the solving of the clues is only the beginning. It is the only crossword that has required solvers to cut the completed grid into an origami wren, an advent calendar, or a snowflake—and those are just three examples from its Christmassy themes. Other themes are less physical but no less involving.

"Be prepared," warned Sondheim, "for odd shapes, sizes and problems." And while his own *Listener*-style puzzles cannot be faulted on the grounds of wit, ingenuity, or addictiveness, they were a big ask.

To introduce newcomers to the delights of the British cryptic with *Listener*-style puzzles is a little like persuading people to take a pleasurable healthy stroll on the weekends by dropping them blindfolded into the Borneo jungle equipped with a butter knife for hacking through the undergrowth. But you can't blame Sondheim for trying.

(If you remain tempted, the nuts and bolts of the more straightforward British cryptic follow. Soon, "Poetical scene with surprisingly chaste Lord Archer vegetating [3, 3, 8, 12]" will yield its secret . . .)

PASTIME THAT BRITS KEEP SECRET?

CRYPTIC

A rudimentary tool kit for solving British puzzles

The relentlessly inventive constructor Brendan Emmett Quigley told *The New York Times* in 2013 of his predilection for cryptic crosswords. Not only do cryptics dominate his solving time, he said, they also have made his construction more playful:

> *The cryptic bug has forced me to anagram words I would normally never have bothered to anagram, look for words contained in other words, even notice words running backward.*

There's still another reason for trying out the strange British form. I maintain that cryptic crosswords are easier than their definitional cousins—and I maintain that in the face of goggle-eyed skepticism from those who have seen those odd phrases that don't appear to have anything to do with what anyone might reasonably pencil into their grids.

The reason is this: A cryptic clue typically gives you two routes to the answer. Consider a noncryptic clue like "Disposition (6)." This could be answered by LAYOUT, or MAKEUP, or TEMPER, and there's no way of knowing which the constructor has in mind until you get some letters from another clue—which will itself be subject to the same holdups.

Now imagine that it's a cryptic crossword and that same entry is clued with what is known as **a double definition**: a clue in two handy, interconnecting parts. Let's say "Kind disposition (6)," from the constructor known as Rufus.

There's only one word that fits both halves of the clue once you think of "kind" not as in tenderhearted but as in "What kind of man is this?" and "disposition" straightforwardly, as in "an unfriendly disposition."

So you can write in NATURE without worrying about whether it fits with the other clues—although it would be a shame not to linger for a moment on the pleasing surface reading: the welcome sight of someone who is going to be nice to you. And this is pretty much as short as cryptic clues get: As you'll see, longer ones start to tell miniature stories, or present you with endearingly daffy imagery.

More importantly, you don't have to worry as much about the grid: You have a sense when you've cracked each clue, without having to see whether the option you've chosen is going to mess up the interlocking entries. In a cryptic, each clue is a miniature puzzle in itself.

This was the goal of those eccentrics who developed the cryptic form in the Britain of the 1930s. As we saw earlier, the posher British newspapers had waged a campaign against the crossword when it arrived from America; when they performed an about-face, they at least had the decency to come up with something a little different to print in their pages.

Happily, they were able to call on the services of people like Edward Powys Mathers (1892–1939), a poet and translator who liked crosswords well enough but worried that they were too repetitive "to hold for long the attention of anyone concerned with and interested in words." (He chose the name of the Spanish Grand Inquisitor Torquemada as his nom de guerre, and as we'll see, most British constructors operate under mysterious pseudonyms.)

Hence clues like the spoonerism, and indeed the double definition: There is a pleasure in seeing how two bits of language with apparently unconnected senses can each lead entirely fairly to the answer.

If you can see how "Quits flat" works, you've got the hang of the double definition. Two more:

Boat put in water (6)
Very exciting, filthy habit (4-6)

From the constructor known as Virgilius, the first is LAUNCH (a noun and then a verb); the second, by Paul, is NAILBITING (adjective, then noun).

The next weapon in your tool kit is the **cryptic definition**. In a typical cryptic clue, you find a definition of the answer at the beginning or the end of the clue; here you get another one making up the rest, like in the double definitions above—but things are a little more playful. These are kindred spirits to the clues in American puzzles that end with a question mark and suggest something allusive is going on.

So, in "Savagely competitive boxer getting to do more than bite his opponent? (3-3-3)," the first two words are the definition of DOGEATDOG and the rest is a more picturesque route to the same destination. The fact that you will inevitably read "boxer" as a sportsman rather than a canine and spend some time thinking about Evander Holyfield's pinna in Mike Tyson's buccal cavity is part of the fun.

Here is another couple. If they don't yield, having a look at the answer and working backward is just as good a way of grasping how it all works.

Remember Pooh's imaginary? (4,2,4)
Unfathomable, not like A Midsummer Night's Dream (10)

So these are BEARINMIND, by Orlando, and BOTTOMLESS from the London *Times*, the constructors for which are anonymous.

Most often, the definition part of the clue is coupled with something that asks you to move letters around to find the answer, often an **anagram**. In such clues, you are given—though it is not obvious which is which—a definition of the answer, an indication that you should be jumbling some letters, and precisely those letters that need jumbling.

That indication could be anything that suggests change:

movement, disorder, or even drunkenness. So in Notabilis's clue "President's unexpected vote loser (9)," "unexpected" tells you to scramble "vote loser" for President ROOSEVELT.

More anagrams:

Strange I should tan poorly (10)
Demand to rewrite scenes in it (10)

The first, by Puck, is an anagram ("poorly") of "I should tan": OUTLANDISH. The second, by Mudd, is an anagram ("to rewrite") of "scenes in it": INSISTENCE. Not too fiendish, are they?

Even less Mephistophelian is the **hidden answer**. Here, again, there's a definition at either the beginning or the end of the clue; the rest is made up of a string of words that contain the answer and a hint that this is what's going on.

The pleasure here is in noticing that the answer has been in front of you the whole time, hiding in plain sight. So in the London *Times*'s "Some forget to get here for gathering (3-8)," you're being asked to take "some" of the letters of "forget to get here" for GETTOGETHER.

What's in Latin sign, if I can translate, is of no importance (13)
As seen in jab, reach of pro miserably failing to meet expectations? (6,2,7)

The first, by Brian Greer, is INSIGNIFICANT; the second is from the London *Times*: BREACHOFPROMISE.

As the pioneering cryptic constructor Afrit wrote, the clue

that hides the answer "may be flagrantly misleading, but the solver cannot complain, because there the solution is, staring him in the face." Harsh, but fair.

You're ready now for the information that the hidden word might go backward, like in this clue from *The Sunday Telegraph*: "Cooking equipment taken back from heiress I tormented (10)." Same principle, but "taken back from" means we read some of the letters of "heiress I tormented" in reverse order for ROTISSERIE.

I am not going to pretend every clue contains each of the letters of the answer. No, other times, you're asked to come up with one word and then write that one backward: the **reversal**. Here you find a definition of the answer; as you must be expecting by now, a hint to another word; and an instruction to write that one backward to find the answer a second time.

So it is in this clue, from a qualifying puzzle for the London *Times*'s crossword championship: "Grass one should put back, and maybe does (4)." Here, you use "Grass" to summon up the word REED and write it backward for the answer DEER, noticing in passing that "does" is one of those words whose relevant sense is not always immediately apparent.

And again:

A delay held back a sporting event (4)
Advanced from the right with others (2,2)

The first clue is Jed's: You put back "a lag" for GALA. The second is from the London *Times*: "late," spelled from right to left, gives you ET AL.

Other times, these words you come up with are written in the normal direction, but there are more than one of them, in a kind of clue known by aficionados as a **charade**, after a tiresome parlor game that need not detain us.

So when Quixote asks for "Student seen as 'home bird' (6)," he wants you to take a word for being "home" (in, as in "I stayed in all evening") and combine it with a kind of "bird" (the tern) to make up a student: INTERN.

A couple of other clues that are just one thing after another:

Players below par no longer wanted (4-3)
Carol thus delivered girls' beach wear (10)

The players on a stage plus something that's a bit "off" give us CASTOFF in the first, from Orlando; the other, by Paul, asks you to combine SUNG and LASSES for SUNGLASSES. In a variant of this type of clue, you might be asked to put one of the words *inside* the other—same principle.

Right, two more devices and you should be ready to solve. Clues that use **soundalikes** give you a definition at one end or the other, plus a word or phrase and a suggestion that you conjure up another word or phrase that sounds the same. "Excited as Oscar's announced (4)," from *The Sunday Telegraph*, for instance, asks you to think of a well-known playwright called Oscar and then write in the synonym for "excited" that sounds the same: WILD. The hint that there's a homophone can be anything that involves speaking or hearing:

Musical work that's melodious to the ear (5)
Mentioned pet getting soft drinks (5)

So that's SUITE (which Chifonie says sounds like "sweet") and COKES ("coax," according to *The Sunday Times*).

Finally, a form of wordplay that, we will recall, goes back to ancient prophecies scribbled on leaves. Yes, it's the **acrostic**, in which you take the initial letters of a run of words in the clue to match the definition. In Orlando's "Black and white lamb starts to cry (4)," you need the "starts" of "Black and white lamb" for a synonym of "cry," BAWL.

Likewise:

Does he lead prayer for openers? Is Mohammed a Muslim? (4)
Natty, elegant and trim, primarily (4)

The first is by Bunthorne and gives us IMAM; the second is by Viking and gives us NEAT.

But where, the more diligent reader might be wondering, is the definition in the clue for NEAT? Once you remove the wordplay ("Natty, elegant and trim, primarily"), all you're left with is a little number four in brackets. But at the same time, that wordplay is in itself a fair definition of NEAT. Very occasionally, the cryptic solver comes across an all-in-one clue like this. One that uses the "hidden answer" device, by Mudd, is "Some hitman in Japan? (5)," where you take "some" of "hitman in Japan" for NINJA.

Our last examples, both anagrams:

Royal at one time—aren't I spoiled! (5,10)
Punctuation mark perhaps too freely used (10)

A pithy description from Paul of MARIEANTOINETTE and a mild admonition from Rufus about the misplaced APOSTROPHE.

That's it. You're a solver. Go and buy a newspaper or spark up your web browser. Most of the clues in its puzzle should yield once you've set about them with the tools given above in some combination or other, twisted to produce surface readings in each clue that point you in the wrong direction. Your job is to enjoy—perhaps with a friend or relative—puzzling out what's really being said. You now know everything the constructor does.

And as for that "Poetical scene with surprisingly chaste Lord Archer vegetating (3, 3, 8, 12)"—a little cultural knowledge is needed for this one. Lord Archer is a British politician accused by a newspaper of having had sex with a prostitute. He won substantial damages, but suspicions lingered, made worse by his party's campaigning for Victorian-style family values. He and his wife live in a building called the Old Vicarage, Grantchester, which further upset his critics because it is the former home of Rupert Brooke, whose much-loved poem of the same name is a nostalgic, patriotic favorite. Just when Archer's rise seemed unstoppable, he was found to have lied in court about the prostitution business, was banished from public life, and went home to lick his wounds.

And so when the retired churchman John Graham, better known as the constructor Araucaria, wrote the clue "Poetical scene with surprisingly chaste Lord Archer vegetating (3, 3, 8, 12)"—a lovely long anagram of THEOLDVICARAGEGRANTCHESTER—solvers found their pent-up indignation regarding

Archer expressed with wit and economy in an ingenious and memorable eight-word rebuke.

Such specific knowledge is rarely necessary to solve a British cryptic; still, since British cultural references may well be too much to take on in combination with a new kind of puzzle, American solvers are better advised to seek out the cryptics in *The Wall Street Journal* (on Saturdays), *The New York Times* (every few Sundays), and consistently in *The Nation*, which is even known to be bought reluctantly by conservative solvers who come for the puzzle and avert their eyes from the politics.

(And if you haven't scurried away in search of a cryptic—or if you've just returned from a successful solve—we move now from Across to Down. What happens to crossword puzzles when they are released into the world . . . ?)

PART TWO

DOWN

CHEATING—VOTING TWICE?

DOUBLE-CROSSING

What constitutes cheating in crosswords?

In the *Friends* episode "The One with the Dirty Girl," Rachel announces that she really wants to finish a crossword entirely by herself. But she is later heard suggesting to Chandler a trip to see a musical—specifically, and, more to the point, suspiciously, the 1996 Tony Award winner. She adds innocently that she is sure it must be good and casually asks if Chandler happens to know its name. (Spoiler alert: Rachel eventually completes the puzzle.)

Was Rachel cheating? The only real answer: That is entirely a matter for her own judgment.

There's a sliding scale from sinlessness to sinfulness when it comes to filling a grid. The purest solve involves nothing more than the newspaper, a pen or pencil, and a solitary solver. It's one-on-one combat, unarmed. No reference books, no phone-a-friend, and certainly no Internet. Anything that deviates in the merest morsel from this monastic model is, for some, cheating.

Outside of competitive solving, which we will examine below, crosswords aren't issued with terms of engagement. There're no Marquess of Queensberry rules for wordplay. By definition, you can't cheat when there are no rules, but most solvers have a sense—perhaps not articulated but running deep within them—of what is Acceptable and what is Unacceptable when they sit down and peer at 1 across.

These boundaries of fair play vary, as do the settings in which solvers solve. Some approach puzzles in pairs, as is their right, and even if you're going it alone, you may or may not choose to make judicious calls on those around you. Rachel initially plans to solve without that help but shifts the rules as the solve reveals itself to be more challenging.

That kind of moral mission drift is familiar and can take place in the course of a single puzzle. If you were to respond to the very first clue you looked at by pulling *Roget's Thesaurus* from the bookshelf, an onlooker would be entirely justified in asking what exactly was the point of the exercise and whether you had the slightest grasp of what the pleasure of the puzzle is supposed to be.

When it comes to the endgame, by contrast, you might be looking at a grid with a dusting of unfilled squares and a couple of clues that stubbornly refuse to budge. Then it's decision time. If you've set yourself, explicitly or otherwise, the challenge of completing the puzzle using your brain alone, then you must gather your strength and return to rereading every word of the clue, saying aloud the letters provided by the others to try and elicit a plausible answer, paying no heed the concerns of those around you, listening to your apparently deranged mumbling.

But then again—again—nobody has imposed those boundaries on you, and you may prefer to use an external source to find some synonyms, finish the exercise, and get on with the rest of your life, or get off the bus before you miss your stop.

The rules may change over a lifetime of solving, too. An experienced solver expects most of the action to take place in his or her head. For a beginner, it's game on by any means necessary. Yes, the constructor is aiming to lose gracefully and intends you to decrypt every clue. But that doesn't mean that the crossword should simply crumble before the novice. There has to be a degree of bloodshed.

To tackle a crossword is to enjoy the experience of your brain pulling on many different areas simultaneously, working in a way that everyday life rarely calls for. It is also a matter of conventions: of coming to know those words that, as we saw earlier, appear more often in puzzles than in real life. Until recently, the best way for beginners to understand the clues that defeated them was to buy the following day's edition of the paper and look at the answers; today, the paper's website may offer a cheat button for individual clues or the whole solution on the day of publication.

It may be educative, but the key thing is not to say, "Oh yes, it was WEBPAGES," but instead to take the time to see how "Safari sights" cunningly put the name of the web browser at the beginning of the clue to disguise its capital S and to make a note to look out for that trick the next time you encounter it. This is not just about the moment of revelation: It is about the future of your solving soul. As each such device becomes clearer to you, your pleasure in future puzzles will multiply. If you remain baffled, most crosswords have dedicated blogs where other solvers parse each answer, so enlightenment is never that far away.

Now, what if you have never heard of the word that you missed? Well, you look it up. But what if you haven't admitted defeat, not quite yet? You have a guess, you feel confident it fits the clue and the crossing letters, but you have no way of knowing for sure—is it OK to consult a dictionary at this point?

Once more, it depends who you ask.

Some see the looking up of words as laudable and a sign that the solver is increasing his or her word power—and, after all, some newspapers give dictionaries as prizes for solving, and they can hardly expect solvers not to use them. Others regard a trip to the reference shelves as a sign of the coming apocalypse—and they took that view even when dictionaries were all made of paper and required a little donkeywork to obtain the answer.

Nowadays, the nearest dictionary might be online or on a smartphone, in which case it may offer help of a kind way beyond the powers of a traditional reference work. With the bound, paper variety of dictionary, you need at least to be able to guess how a word begins in order to look it up and see if it's right; a digital source that allows you to use wildcards lets you type in ?H?R?A?A? and confirms in seconds that you are a CHARLATAN.

But are you? Your sense of what is and is not fair is a declaration of self: of how you prefer to reach goals and what you like to do with your own mind. As the former *New York Times* puzzle editor Will Weng used to say: It's your puzzle. Solve it any way you want.

Some take that advice quite literally. In Alan Hollinghurst's novel *The Swimming-Pool Library*, the narrator William Beckwith tries to finish a puzzle begun by an elderly aristocrat, but isn't sure that some of the words in the grid are correct. "Oh, I don't do the *clues*," chuckles Lord Nantwich, explaining that he plays a kind of solitaire in which he has to fill the grid with interlocking words that are *not* the answers.

"Often, I'm afraid," he explains, "you get buggered in the last corner." Indeed. But William and the baron enjoy themselves inventing such words as CO-ZIP (to fasten your pants with someone else's help)—and who is to deny them that? At least they're fictional. Nobody would do such a thing in real life. Would they?

One real-life crossword fanatic was the stalwart English actor John Gielgud. He wrote to the London *Times*'s crossword editor in 1993 to say that his puzzle addiction began in 1944, inspired by an electrician at the Haymarket Theatre: "I have found the crossword a sovereign therapy during endless hours of waiting while filming and doing television."

His approach to filling the grid, however, was not always sovereign. Fellow actor David Dodimead once noticed that Gielgud was "skipping through the clues, neatly filling them in at an amazing pace."

Was there nothing the great man couldn't do? Dodimead scanned Gielgud's grid and found his eye drawn to one entry in particular. "Excuse me, John," he asked, "what are DIDDYBUMS?"

"No idea," replied Gielgud. "But it does fit awfully well."

(The idea that you are only cheating yourself is wedded to the notion that crossword puzzles must be good for you. If they give you pleasure, then they surely are good for you, but sometimes the claims are greater—that crosswords will prolong the life of your brain. Really . . . ?)

CRAZY TO BE SEEN IN GEORGIA, TWICE?

GAGA

Do crosswords stave off dementia?

If you want to lend a character in a film or TV program an intelligent air, give him or her a crossword. The puzzle serves as shorthand for a vague cluster of cleverness indicators, such as impressive powers of recall, sizable vocabulary, and perhaps speedy lateral thinking.

One link between crosswords and the brain that everyone seems certain about is that they yield greater dividends the older you get: A puzzle a day keeps dementia at bay. Well, that's not quite "certain," I think to myself as I wander over to the corner of an Oxford pub toward the waiting psychologist investigating the link between crosswords and mental acuity, but certainly many people know an elderly relative who does a puzzle every morning and still has all his or her faculties.

Sitting by the restrooms, I strap on a pair of noise-reduction headphones and begin the psychological test.

Kathryn Friedlander and her colleague Philip Fine are interested in solvers' cognitive skills and motivational drivers. She has joined a weekly get-together for constructors, solvers, and crossword bloggers that takes place around the UK every Saturday. It started when the constructor John Henderson (Enigmatist, who has been constructing for *The Guardian* since he was fifteen years old) noticed that whenever he solved in a pub, others were looking over his shoulder, and decided against a festering annoyance and in favor of actively inviting others to join him.

This week, those others include Kathryn, who wants to be around crossworders so that she can gather some data. She has devised a series of exercises for three groups: solvers, expert solvers, and noncrossworders. I am invited to count the number of vowels in various words, then fill in the blanks in some others. I suspect that the first task is designed to hobble me in the second by planting in my head various unhelpful linguistic shapes and sounds. The research is ongoing, but I learn something about myself, and not something flattering: While I appreciate that the point of the exercise is academic enrichment, I find that I urgently want to get a decent "score."

Afterward, we chat about Kathryn's curiosity regarding whether very able solvers have higher "fluid intelligence"—the capacity to approach new problems with a fresh mind and apply the appropriate analysis. The tasks have been designed to give her a sense of what's happening in the brain when it is led to a misleading place, then recovers its bearings and enjoys what the crossword world calls the "penny-drop" moment of clarity. For me, at least, I tell her, there's an addictive quality to the experience of letting go of the apparent meaning of a clue and seeing the message hidden in code that leads to the real interpretation.

We discuss a paper with the title "Eye-Witnesses Should Not Do Cryptic Crosswords Prior to Identity Parades" from the journal *Perception*, which concludes that solving a cryptic has a detrimental effect on subsequent face recognition, and that the same does not go for quick crosswords, reading, or sudoku. It's a convincing piece of research that presents its results cleanly and without undue speculation as to the reasons behind them. I ask Kathryn whether she has come across any similarly decent investigations into whether crosswords are good for older people's minds. There's not much in the papers, in the sense of peer-reviewed journals, but there's plenty in the other sort of papers: tips such as 10 WAYS TO DECREASE ALZHEIMER'S RISK: FLEX THAT BRAINPOWER—DO CROSSWORD PUZZLES, or PUZZLES AND EXERCISE HELP BEAT DEMENTIA SYMPTOMS, SAY EXPERTS.

Ah, those much-vaunted "experts." It's from the newspapers that people I know—relatives and coworkers—have got the idea that crosswords are a prophylactic against Alzheimer's. Newspapers are of course also the place where crosswords are most readily available, so the association is presumably good for circulation. In the twenty-first century, similar pieces began to appear about the benefits of the fourth estate's newer geegaw, the sudoku.

There are more such articles every couple of months, and if the combined reports are to be believed, here's the truth about crosswords: Solving is a handy way of hanging on to your faculties, but this comes at a cost. And the price is paid by your waistline. In 2009 there was a flurry of stories warning that solving puzzles makes you fat, citing research by Dr. Kathleen Martin Ginis of Ontario into whether exercising willpower in one activity leaves less resolve when you approach others.

Since solving is often a seated pastime, it's not difficult to visualize a connection between crosswords and gastric girth—and the same goes for the idea that crosswords are a kind of brain-saving mental workout. You can see vividly how both claims might be true. Alternatively, they might both be false. Or they might be neither, in the sense that nobody has actually tested either.

In the case of the crossword obesity epidemic, it's the last of those options. Ginis's research didn't include any sudokus or crosswords. "Someone told me that the story had been in the UK press," she told the BBC. "I was quite excited. I googled it, I saw it, and I just cringed. I felt sick."

Probe too deeply into the evidence for stories that use words like "neurobics" and "brainercise," and you'll find yourself similarly baffled and confounded. Here's the clearest statement I've seen about the facts of the matter. It's from a 1999 paper in the *Journal of Experimental Psychology* called "Predictors of Crossword Puzzle Proficiency and Moderators of Age-Cognition Relations," and it is, to say the least, deflating: "The results provide no evidence to suggest that amount of crossword puzzle experience reduces age-related decreases in fluid cognition or enhances age-related increases in crystallized cognition." In other words, solve if you like, but don't think it will stop you going gaga.

Kathryn's experience is similar. Crosswords may or may not have these beneficial effects but the evidence isn't there to tell us much. Besides, she adds, what aspects of which kind of crossword are we talking about?

Some elements of solving—synonyms, say, antonyms, and abbreviations—are correlated with regular solving, but may also improve with age, whether you solve or not. Others—preserving ambiguities, switching from the big picture to the details—decline. Doing crosswords makes you better at doing crosswords, but that's not such an exciting discovery. A proper examination of popular computer games with names like *Professor Okinaga's Cerebral Zumba* revealed that users are no better at memory, concentration, planning, or problem solving than nonusers; what these programs do is make you good at the next volume you buy of *Professor Okinaga's Cerebral Zumba*, and there's no reason to believe that the same is not the case with crosswords.

And what of the real-world anecdotal examples: the avidly solving relatives who have retained their marbles? Can we say with any certainty whether the solving is the cause of the retention of marbles, or the retention of marbles the cause of the solving, or whether both share an earlier cause? Crucially, I'd like to know more about whether this relative solves alone or with a friend or relative.

Kathryn is more open to the idea that cosolving might have benefits for the elderly, and she is not alone in her interest in the social angle. I'd recommend crosswords over sudokus as a morning activity in the Rusty Cogs Retirement Home on the basis that you're less likely to call out an interesting sudoku column for everyone to enjoy or to find yourself inspired to relate an anecdote on the basis of an especially amusing 7 in that day's grid. Whatever puzzle you choose, a daily challenge that offers temporary goals and some pleasure is not a bad thing; as a cheap way of dealing with mental-health problems in an aging population, however, it may not be enough.

The image of crosswords as intrinsic Alzheimer's bashers seems unlikely to go away anytime soon. For one thing, there's the legacy of the notion that you have to be particularly intelligent to solve a crossword.

For another, the association has a distinct appeal for constructors and solvers, both of whom are often asked to explain why on earth they channel their time and energy into puzzles. "Still, it staves off dementia, I suppose" lets them off the hook. But the implicit charge—that crosswords are a waste of time—should not need to be countered. There's no real comfort in seeing the newspapers that decried the arrival of the crossword in the 1920s and proscribed their use on grim utilitarian grounds now prescribing their use on a similarly dispiriting cost-benefit basis.

And so I leave Kathryn to her research and look back across the pub to the gathered solvers, all of whom are there because it's a congenial way to spend an afternoon and an opportunity to have a stiff word or two with the constructors of some recent troublesome clues. That's an end in itself. If you want to do a puzzle, you don't need a doctor's note.

(So if the puzzle appears to be taking longer than usual, you don't need to fear for your mental capacity. Besides, what are you doing timing your solve, anyway . . . ?)

FAST

The urge to time your solve

Got up
Had shave
Did Times *crossword*
Had another shave

—ROGER McGOUGH

The wonderful 2006 documentary about crosswords, *Wordplay*, shows us two very different worlds. There are the famous solvers—Bill Clinton, Jon Stewart, Mike Mussina—and those who are not so renowned outside crosswording circles. Or you might think of the same two groups as the casual puzzle fans, who grab a crossword when they can, and the devotees, who see each puzzle as training for the annual American Crossword Puzzle Tournament, in which they will race other super-solvers at the Marriott hotel in Stamford, Connecticut, each year.

I see them differently. I see the happy solvers and the damned.

Clinton, Stewart, Mussina, and the others smile as they describe their relationships with the grid—in these moments, it is a movie about pleasure. In invidious contrast are the faces of the time-obsessed entrants, in particular that of the astonishingly gifted Al Sanders.

The movie follows Sanders and other contestants as they prepare for and then attend the twenty-eighth tournament. The viewer might well wish that he or she were there, too. It's a weekend away from everything except puzzles: collegiate, mutually supportive, occasionally silly, and always proud. Yes, it's an alluring world—except for the actual business of the timed tournament puzzles.

Al Sanders makes it to the final. He looks every inch the winner. And, in fact, he finishes first—but after he announces "done," he notices that he has omitted to fill in two squares. The shots of the moment of realization—Sanders hurling his noise-reduction headphones to the floor, then gasping, red-faced and bent double—are heartrending. But they are also evidence of the inevitable result of timing crosswords.

You see the same thing in a book by solver Marc Romano called *Crossworld: One Man's Journey into America's Crossword Obsession*. Romano enters the American Crossword Puzzle Tournament, and his is a tale of anxiety, apprehension, and anguish that ends with the competition wreaking psychological and physical havoc as he collapses at home, a broken man.

It's the same at the British equivalent, the *Times* Crossword Championship. There, the winner is the same man every year, a finance director called Mark Goodliffe. His solving is enjoyable from afar—losing some valuable seconds considering whether RAISINY is a word before returning to his relentless decryption of cryptics. More enjoyable, though, is the annual response from perennial runner-up Peter Brooksbank.

Goodliffe skipped the 2007 final because his wife had given birth two days before. Brooksbank quipped: "If he could be persuaded to have another one, that would be useful." A later wheeze, to create a distraction: "You could slip a mobile phone into his pocket and get someone to phone it." In 2010 he was terser: "I'm going to have to kill him."

These are gags, but ones delivered through gritted teeth. They are also a warning not to get involved. Usain Bolt might be able to run the 100 meters in 9.58 seconds, but that doesn't mean there's no point in the rest of us ever exercising. Indeed, since the constructor of a puzzle has slaved so long over its intricacies, it seems disrespectful to plow away, giving only the minimum possible attention to each clue. Sometimes, though, the temptation is there.

For one thing, if a solve is going fast, you feel smart. At this moment, it might be worth recalling the thoughts of the humorist Stephen Fry, often described as "a man with a brain the size of Kent." (Kent is a county of approximately 923,000 acres.) "I don't know many people who can do the *Times* crossword more quickly than me," Fry notes in his first autobiography. "There again I do know dozens and dozens of people vastly more intelligent than me for whom the simplest cryptic clue is a mystery—and one they are not in the least interested in penetrating."

So, horses for courses. But another temptation comes from the little clocks that accompany many newspapers' puzzles in their online versions. Some are even set to time your solve by default, making speed seem an intrinsic part of the process. Again, though, there is something to bear in mind.

These digital versions of the puzzles typically provide leaderboards that purport to show which solvers have been especially speedy tackling each puzzle. The problem, though, is that the times at the top tend to be implausibly low. Not even implausible on the level of an Al Sanders or a Mark Goodliffe—these are times so low you wonder whether the solver has had time to read the clues. And, of course, they have not. These are people, you suspect, who, for reasons best known to themselves, have completed the puzzle in advance—perhaps on paper, or using another login—and then simply typed the answers in order to appear to be cruciverbally superhuman. And since their times are quite literally measures of nothing, what does yours mean in relation to them?

I concede, though, that the temptation is sometimes irresistible. Indeed, even the sight of the near-broken Sanders was no deterrent, and since the release of *Wordplay*, the American Crossword Puzzle Tournament has seen such an increase in attendance that it has moved to a larger Marriott, near Brooklyn Bridge.

If you must concentrate on speed, then, here are some tips.

> Train yourself in a kind of automatic writing so that you can use those scribbling seconds to start reading the next clue.

Reshape your Es. In his book, Marc Romano reveals that Will Shortz advised him that modifying his handwriting has saved him "time both in solving and in life." Restructure your script around fast strokes of the pencil.

Have someone tell you a joke before you start solving. Neuroscientist Mark Beeman found that college students performed better at word-association puzzles if they had been shown a video of stand-up comedy beforehand than if they had watched something boring or scary.

Use a pencil and an eraser. *Times* Championship winner Peter Biddlecombe adds: "If you think that a letter is unclear, be prepared to rub it out and write it again." No pen.

Start in the bottom right-hand corner. Some champions swear by this technique, on the basis that the constructor may have written those clues last, in a more tired frame of mind.

Try to get the beginnings, not the ends, of words—beginnings have more variation and yield their secrets faster.

Check. As Will Shortz said in his welcome to the twenty-eighth American Crossword Puzzle Tournament: "If either you leave a letter out or you make a mistake, that will

> cost you 195 points. The champions generally spend a little extra time after they finish a puzzle, looking it over, making sure that every square is filled and that nothing silly has been put in a square." And if you are merely timing yourself for fun, you haven't finished at all if there's a single misplaced letter. Your time is, sadly, infinity. Check again.

But be aware that you are making sacrifices. Not least among them is the potential crosswords offer to have the opposite effect to that of a stopwatch—to make you *less* aware of time. The moments you spend in a puzzle have the potential to shut out the outside world for a blessedly silent period. After a more leisurely solve, you return refreshed from a happier place where, unlike the rest of life, the day is not carved up into fifteen-minute segments, each of which must be accounted for. The other, realer problems in your life are easier to solve.

(Although any exhortation that you shut out the rest of your life while solving should come with a health warning . . .)

THE SOUND OF *WEBSTER'S*, UP TO A POINT?

ADDICTION

When crosswords prove too much of a distraction

In the wine-themed road trip movie *Sideways*, we see Miles Raymond solve—in pen—two real-word *New York Times* puzzles, set by Alan Arbesfeld and Craig Kasper. The viewer is taken aback by the incorrigible Miles's drink-driving, but that pales into insignificance when we see him indulging in a spot of what might be termed solve-driving. Here is a man with some unusual priorities. Miles is not, though, cinema's greatest exemplar of the Man Who Loves Puzzles Too Much.

For that, we turn instead to the classic British weepie *Brief Encounter*, its screenplay written by Noël Coward and based on his one-act play *Still Life*. In the stage version, housewife Laura Jesson is tempted to enter into an extramarital affair with charming physician Alec Harvey and all the action takes place in the refreshment room of Milford Junction railway station.

The screen adaptation shows us Laura's home life. Crucially, her husband, Fred, is not portrayed as a monster; neither is Dr. Harvey a baddie. No, Fred is a kind and decent man: The villain in *Brief Encounter* is a crossword.

Consider the first time we see the married couple together. Fred invites Laura to sit by the fire and help him with the *Times* crossword; she replies that he has the most peculiar ideas of relaxation.

"Fred," mutters the viewer, "can't you see that your wife is forcing that smile? The last thing she wants is to listen to you calling out clues." Yet, in the very next scene, he asks Laura to complete the Keats line "When I behold, upon the night's starr'd face, huge cloudy symbols of a high . . ."

With an effort, Laura gives the answer, ROMANCE, and

suggests that Fred check it in *The Oxford Book of English Verse*—he doesn't: He's satisfied because it fits with the entries DELIRIUM and BALUCHISTAN.

"Romance!" barks the viewer. "Romance, Fred, you damned fool! Not the word 'romance'; not the seven-letter string R-O-M-A-N-C-E: It's the real thing your wife is crying out for!"

Here the film declares that crosswords are a retreat from the world and from feeling—an abstraction perhaps not dangerous in itself but to be feared in that it ultimately sends respectable wives into the arms of strangers in railway refreshment rooms.

"And is it any wonder?" yells the viewer, now distraught. "I'll tell you who wouldn't spend time with Laura working out which words fit with BALUCHISTAN. Dr. Alec Harvey, that's who. The Dr. Alec Harvey who's been making her faint, that's who. Out-of-season rowing in astonishing scenes in a botanical garden is Alec's idea of fun, being stranded in the water, helpless with laughter—not filling a monotone grid with the names of Pakistani provinces."

And it gets worse. One evening Laura blurts out that she had lunch earlier with a strange man, and that he took her to the movies. Concentrating on his puzzle, Fred replies, "Good for you," and goes back to pondering who said, "My kingdom for a horse."

Such is the grip of the puzzle on Fred's mind that he moves on to his next clue rather than addressing the reality of his marriage crumbling in front of him. Just as *Scarface* had cocaine and *Trainspotting* had heroin, so *Brief Encounter* shows the harrowing effects of crossword addiction.

"For God's sake, Fred!" the viewer is by now howling. "Put down that newspaper and hold her in your arms!"

Happily, in the closing scene, he does. It is only as the picture ends that we see the villain—this scourge of respectable middle-class marriage, this divisive word game—vanquished. Laura's anguish is so intense that Fred, finally, lets go of his copy of *The Times*, places it beside him on the sofa, and tells her, "You've been a long way away," adding, unbearably, "Thank you for coming back to me."

What gives *Brief Encounter* its power is not what is said but what is not said: Fred's declaration—unspoken, but no less unsentimental for that—that he is giving up the evil of crosswords. That his very English repression prevents him from saying this outright makes the denouement all the more moving.

(Better, always, to let the one you love take part in the filling of the grid . . .)

SOUNDS LIKE A FIGHT, FOR TWO PEOPLE?

DUAL

Solving need not be solitary

The crossword has long been allied to its cousin in modernity, public transport. When the 1920s craze was at its most frenzied, the Baltimore and Ohio Railroad furnished its mainline trains with dictionaries. And the Pennsylvania Railroad went one better than the B&O, printing crosswords on the menus in the dining car.

The commuter has a period of forced inactivity, but he also has the newspaper, which contains within it as good a way as any of whiling away the journey. A quiet time of contemplation. Indeed, the commuter or traveler, locked into solitary battle with a constructor, is one of the most enduring images of crosswording. As puzzle addict Marc Romano wrote in his book *Crossworld*, a journey . . .

is made immeasurably better if you have a collection of Brendan Emmett Quigley crosswords to battle your way through while you're in tedious transit; the hours literally pass like minutes.

Need the battle, though, be solitary? Surely those 1920s dictionaries led to conversations—and perhaps more? In the 1925 comic film *The Freshman* Harold Lloyd is introduced to love interest Peggy in a scene where they peer at "number nineteen vertical—a name for the one you love," and the two are soon billing SWEETHEART and cooing HONEYBUNCH to each other as they attempt to solve the clue, and so true love is born.

Even in the more formal environment of the British commuter train, the clue could provide social glue. A gentleman who identified himself as "8.4 AM" wrote to the London *Times* in 1934 to describe how he and his fellow passengers attempted to complete the puzzle between Shenfield and Romford. "Team spirit is essential," he explains, and his team is structured around the analogy of a soccer side. The "center-forward" is a clerk "unerring in his spelling"; the "outside-right," an expert in anagrams and farming terms, and the "outside-left" is "only included for the 'remains of a classical education,' and because he buys the paper."

And outside of the first-class rail compartment, the image of the solitary solver just doesn't hold up. Consider this: Crosswords are not published with a how-to manual. Guides are available, but when you're tackling your first puzzle, it's unlikely you'll be in a bookshop and instantly drawn to buy one.

Crosswording is most often learned from another person, under the guidance of someone who happens to be around: It's intimate, collaborative, and fun. This is the best way to get to grips with the conventions and quirks of solving: Engage somebody you trust to dispel the fog of intimidation.

Take constructors. When they are asked how they got into puzzles, more often than not the answer goes along the lines of watching a mother or father (or both) solving, from afar; being invited to help with the odd clue; superseding the parent and becoming the family's super-solver; and going on to make some sort of a living out of it. Without the last two steps, it's a similar story for many solvers.

Crosswords bind families: for example the rhythmic exchange of text messages between geographically distant siblings that accompanies their regular appointment with a weekend puzzle, or the extended clan attempting a group solve of a Christmas special over those postholiday days.

The crossword fits well in any environment in which, like Christmas, people find themselves in the same space for longish periods with little to do. In the *Wordplay* documentary, New York Yankees pitcher Mike Mussina explains that he solves solo from October to March but puzzles are for him really a ball season thing:

> *Sometimes we'll sit down as a group and try to plow through it as fast as we can. Whoever's doing the writing doesn't even get to look at the clues. They're writing so fast because of the people leaning over their shoulder firing out answers.*

So it is with musicians, actors, and anyone else whose working life involves as much waiting around as it does actual working. Still the image persists of the solver as isolated—even, sometimes, eccentric.

In the 2009 romcom *All About Steve* the audience learns quickly that Sandra Bullock's awkward lead character is socially maladjusted through the giveaway details of her (a) being a constructor of puzzles and (b)—the clincher—believing that crosswords are "better than life." Her best friend is a hamster. That says it all: Some writers of fiction can have a tendency to use "crosswords" as shorthand for "oddball" or "loner."

Happily, flesh-and-blood solvers are closer to Harold Lloyd and his sweetheart than they are to Bullock's character, who spends the ninety-eight minutes of the movie stalking Bradley Cooper across the country

In 2007 Emily Cox and Henry Rathvon, the married couple who set for *The Boston Globe*, were approached by solver Aric Egmont. He had got to know his girlfriend, Jennie Bass, over the course of weekly Sunday solving sessions in a local café. This had begun on their fourth date and, for Alec, it was proof that the couple did not need a big event to enjoy each other's company: It was "a first tiny step toward normalcy." He asked whether a forthcoming *Globe* puzzle might contain some hidden messages meant for Jennie.

Cox and Rathvon were feeling in a romantic mood—and there is surely no more exacting test of a marriage than coconstructing—and the puzzle appeared on September 23. They took care to include themed entries that would not appear too odd to most solvers but that would have a special meaning for Jennie Bass.

That Sunday in the local café Jennie was tickled to find in the grid her boyfriend's surname, and the names of her best friend and sister, but considered it a coincidence until the clue "Macramé artist's proposal" (LETSTIETHEKNOT).

This was just a hint of what was to come. One hundred and eleven across was "Generic proposal," and as they wrote in the answer (WILLYOUMARRYME), Alec went down on one knee. "There was no reason for me to suspect it," recalled Jennie. "Then he got up and came back with a box, and it was pure elation."

That answer was YES. Pay attention, the team behind *All About Steve*: *That*'s a romcom. Lest you think this was a one-off, so many solvers and constructors have published proposal puzzles that Ben Tausig, puzzle editor for the *Onion* spin-off *A.V. Club* wrote in his *Curious History of the Crossword* that his greatest dream "is to construct a breakup puzzle for someone in need of an innovative way to tell their soon-to-be ex that things are over."

(Ah, the crossword. Making connections between solver and constructor, or between solver and solver. What could be more human . . . ?)

PROGRAM

Can computers crack crosswords?

Google Goggles is a tool that allows your smartphone to "see" what's around you—a landmark, say, or a logo—and to search for that thing without the need for language. I vividly remember the first time I saw the software in action. I opened a newspaper on the sudoku page, pointed my cell phone at the page, and took a snapshot. In a matter of seconds, the screen showed a Google-generated image with the puzzle correctly completed. I stared at the image for a moment or two, utterly unflabbergasted.

These moments of gob-unsmacked, wholly plussed non-wonder at Things Computers Can Now Do But Once Couldn't are becoming more frequent as technology bounds along—almost part of everyday life. And sudoku is perhaps one of the least incongruous activities a computer might take a crack at.

If you're a human solving a sudoku, you're essentially slowly working through algorithms colossally better suited to a central processing unit. It's the cognitive equivalent of deciding that machines aren't best placed to handle your e-mail and resolving instead to handwrite a message, walk it across to a Palo Alto server farm, then walk back, before placing it on the desk of your colleague and returning the six feet to your own workstation. Well done, you. Go, human!

With crosswords, it feels different. Solving a crossword makes you feel something. You've combined feats of memory with some lateral thinking and teased out the hidden treasure. It feels creative, thoughtful. It's a little humbling, then, when you see the strides that computers are making as crossword solvers.

Artificial intelligence researchers have long been interested in the crossword as the kind of thing that computers might find challenging—but not necessarily impossible. The most prominent of the current crossword bots is called Dr. Fill (a pun on Phil McGraw's psychology TV show *Dr. Phil*). Dr. Fill was created by former artificial intelligence researcher Matt Ginsberg, who runs algorithms for the US Air Force when he isn't constructing *New York Times* puzzles.

Ginsberg wanted his machine to be portable, so he loaded up a MacBook Pro laptop with the code he'd created. He added preexisting crossword answers dating back to 1990 and chunks of resources such as Wikipedia and the Internet Movie Database, and took it along to the 2012 American Crossword Puzzle Tournament.

Dr. Fill was not an official entrant: One of the requirements for entry to the tournament is that you be a person. If a person had performed the same as Dr. Fill, he or she would have come in 140th—not a bad placing, and one that can only improve as more time and human thought goes into the software.

Ginsberg, though, doesn't think that what Dr. Fill does counts as thinking. It is, he says, a serial business of summoning likely answers and seeing whether they fit with one another. "Thinking" or not, that's a pretty good description of how most humans approach a puzzle. There is, though, something missing from Dr. Fill's approach, something that should become more apparent as it learns from its mistakes—and that's a discipline it's certainly more serious about than many of its biped rivals.

A hint as to what that missing element might be came when the 2012 tournament included an unexpected twist in one of the puzzles, whereby some answers had to be entered unconventionally. A human might wonder for a while what is going on when the answer MOONMISSIONS doesn't seem to fit the squares for "Apollo 11 and 12 [180 degrees]." But once you twig what "180 degrees" is asking for and see that SNOISSIWNOOW fits with the crossing answers, you can enter it with the kind of confidence that a machine isn't going to have unless it's been given a line of code that explicitly says that Ws can be exchanged for Ms under certain conditions.

And while adding such extra possibilities is not an insurmountable technical problem, that moment of realization is where automated solvers currently part company with their flesh-and-blood rivals. For Dr. Fill, this would be merely another device in the armory. For human solvers, there's something endearingly daft about entering an answer the wrong way up, the words hanging upside down like a spaceman on a moon mission.

Computers will make qualitative progress in tone, speed, range, and so on—but there's something spooky about giving them clues whose whole purpose is a silliness and humor that they seem eternally unlikely to be able to enjoy.

Perhaps there's a better job for technology in creating puzzles rather than solving them. While the range of available grids was once determined by the lead blocks from which the squares were printed, that job is now done by the software used by the constructors, editors, and printers of crosswords.

What about the clues? Some take comfort in the assumption that the architectural donkeywork—providing grids and even words to fill them—might be the extent of computers' involvement. In 2003, the former crossword editor of the London *Sunday Times* Barbara Hall told the BBC that she thought a further impediment would be the size of the word bank the machine would require "because there are so many different meanings for one word."

However, in technical terms, there's barely a difference between a "word bank" of a few thousand words and one of a couple of hundred thousand. It would require no ingenious coding to program a computer to fill grids with answers from a list—of which there are plenty available—then clue each with a database of synonyms.

The resulting puzzle would, technically speaking, be a crossword—indeed, some of the shoddier collections in book form give the impression of having been thus compiled. More interesting is the question: Would it satisfy the solver?

The answer, I suspect, is: by no means all of them. As Stanley Newman has remarked, computer-generated puzzles tend to be full of "junk: foreign phrases, weird abbreviations and obscure words so unfamiliar they don't even qualify as crosswordese."

A human constructor is better able to imagine the experience of answering the clues—where the starting points are likely to be and how each solver's unique journey through the grid might unfold. More importantly, the solver of a decent puzzle in a decent paper does not think of the exercise as an abstract means of whiling away some minutes but as a contest between two people, where the solver knows that the constructor has conceived of the grid as a whole, balanced in terms of tone, subject matter, technique, and difficulty.

More importantly, the constructor's role is, in a phrase much beloved in the crosswording world, to "lose gracefully": to guess correctly that the solver will, with enough application, find the wherewithal to topple every clue and fill every square.

Each constructor's idea of what the solver is likely to know differs, based on hunches and experience—and those differences are as good a way as any of defining the varying personalities among constructors. It's with constructors' personalities that solvers make the relationships that keep them coming back. "I beat Fred Piscop today" means something qualitatively different from "I beat Midweek-Bot v2.1." And once a solver has found the newspaper that suits him, he's made a relationship with a kind of gang—and a gang of highly characterful and diverse individuals who share an ethos and an editorial guiding hand.

Construction is regarded by solvers as a kind of authorship, and our relationship with an author is dependent on his or her being a person, too. The editors of the London *Daily Telegraph* discovered this in 1998 when they initiated a scheme to automate crossword production. Humans would still be paid to write clues, but at that point they would enter a database from which each day's puzzle could be assembled.

The ostensible reason was to reduce the frequency with which some words appeared as answers, although there was also an undeniable financial incentive. A core of the constructors refused to play ball and became known as the "*Telegraph* Six." Ruth Crisp (Crispa) gave her withering assessment of the wheeze: "I don't think a crossword done on a computer can possibly compare with one done individually. I have been compiling crosswords for half a century and I think my judgment can be depended on."

The invisible symmetries of human arrangement could not be replicated by machine, she insisted, and Roger Squires (Rufus) predicted that the tone of the resulting puzzles would be "like combining the musical styles of Beethoven and Mozart in the same musical movement." This was all the more telling coming from the constructors for a newspaper that leaves each of its puzzles anonymous.

The paper's deputy editor, Boris Johnson—who has since become the mayor of London—was forced to agree. "In spite of the advantages the computer possesses, the machine has been condemned for a fatal lack of soul," he announced. "The crossword will remain a duel of wits between the individual composer and the solver." Squires responded with a single tart clue—"Submit to pressure and return to base (9)"—and returned to business. The answer? CLIMBDOWN.

(It should be granted, though, that the home of the world's first programmable electronic digital machine was a place rammed with super-solvers . . .)

WHAT DUMB SPIES SEEK?

INTELLIGENCE

When puzzling meets espionage

In March 2013, the National Security Agency released back issues of its in-house magazine, *Cryptolog*. Like every decent publication, *Cryptolog* found space for a crossword, though, being the NSA, it featured a puzzle of the cryptic variety loved by Sondheim. "Telephoned Reagan, we hear, to make pot (8)," for example, is a slightly scurrilous soundalike clue for CAULDRON, and "Traitors see danger all around! (9)" goes, via an anagram, to RENEGADES.

The idea of signals intelligence officers enjoying a stiff puzzling challenge should surprise nobody. Take Meredith Gardner, who, in his retirement, solved the cryptic in the London *Times* every day. In his working life, too, he had a talent for finding a word or phrase hidden in a mass of surrounding text—handy for a US Army code breaker deciphering messages from a

KGB clerk who was thought to be receiving information about the American nuclear program during the Cold War.

A KGB codebook, abandoned in Finland and partially burned, helped him decipher Soviet intelligence reports, and when, in 1946, one contained the name of the leading scientists in the Western project to develop an atomic bomb, the hunt was on for informants at the Los Alamos weapons lab. Gardner deduced that there was a spy among the staff whose wife had a name that was encoded as three characters. These three characters, decrypted, were E—L. He twigged that the missing letter might not actually be a letter but a word that had been assigned its own character because it was frequently used in English. And one of the most frequently used words in English—well, it's been used seven times already in this paragraph, so that would do it: "the."

And so in 1951 began the controversial trial for espionage of Julius Rosenberg and his wife, E-THE-L. Their subsequent execution attracted international concern, especially because it was not clear to what extent Ethel had really been involved, and America was charged by its liberal critics with nuclear hysteria. Gardner regretted Ethel's death in the electric chair; Jean-Paul Sartre went further, describing it as "a legal lynching." Gardner retired in 1972; after his death, his widow said that her husband's take was that "those people at least believed in what they were doing": not an endorsement of the Rosenbergs but not entirely supportive of their fate, either. Putting aside the ethics of geopolitics, one lesson is clear: Don't work in the world of spying if your name can be rendered as a cryptic clue, and especially if it contains any of the most common English words. Andys, Theos, and Willys—your number's up.

Crosswords and modern Western intelligence agencies came onto the scene in the years just before the First World War; in the Second World War puzzles and spycraft cemented their relationship.

Two years into the Second World War the national British newspaper *The Daily Telegraph* published an unusual letter from a Mr. W. A. J. Gavin, purportedly writing as the chairman of the "Eccentrics Club." A sum of money had been enclosed with the original letter, and the following challenge was issued, with a promise to send the money to a charity if certain conditions were met:

> *If [one of your readers] succeeds in [solving the puzzle] you are authorized to send the enclosed £100 Bank of England note to the Eccentric Club Minesweepers' Fund.*
>
> *My challenge, which allows 12 minutes for a solution, extends to all of your correspondents who claim to do your puzzles in such incredibly short periods of time.*

The editor invited any solvers to come to *The Telegraph*'s Fleet Street offices on a Saturday afternoon. Twelve minutes was an ask, but not impossible—and "Mr. Gavin" never thought it was. The puzzle was solved, the banknote dispatched to the Minesweepers' Fund, and a few weeks later twenty-five of the successful solvers who had turned up on that Saturday afternoon received letters asking them to report to one Colonel Nichols of military intelligence, "who would very much like to see you on a matter of national importance." One of them, Stanley Sedgewick, related what happened when he turned up:

> *I was told, though not so primitively, that chaps with twisted brains like mine might be suitable for a particular type of work as a contribution to the war effort. Thus it was that I reported to "the Spy School" at 1, Albany Road, Bedford.*

The "particular type of work" was code breaking at the new decryption center in Bletchley Park—code breaking that has been judged to have shortened the war "by not less than two years and probably by four years."

And while you would now expect code breaking recruitment to target experts in computing, there was then no programmable electronic digital machine for anyone with that kind of mind to work on. Not, that is, until Bletchley developed just such a device: the Colossus, a looming, loom-size behemoth that was devoted to cryptanalysis of high-level German army communications. Yet, powerful though it was, the human brain was invaluable in peering at encoded messages and spotting the most likely substitutions of words and letter pairs that could wring some sense back into them.

An effective human decrypter had a certain temperament, characterized by meticulousness, the ability to balance ambiguities until they resolved themselves, patience—and a cool head. An unnamed code cracker remembered the necessity of not buckling under pressure:

Just imagine the codework in front of you is a crossword. If you had someone breathing down your neck saying, "You've got to get it done in five minutes," it wouldn't help at all.

The confluence of crosswords, computers, and cryptography makes for a good argument if you ever need to defend the hours you devote to puzzles. "Sure, it may seem like an abstract waste of time," you can say, "but if it was the 1940s, I'd actually be training myself to help prevent the jackboot of Nazi oppression from enslaving all of Europe. Could you just excuse me a moment while I work on this tricky 13 down? Oh, and by the way, do you know what the secret German plan to negotiate a surrender in northern Italy was called?" By the time the other person has looked up that code name and discovered it was Kreuzworträtsel—Operation Crossword—and how arbitrary the name was, you'll have won the argument, or at least had enough uninterrupted time to crack that tricky 13 down.

As well as playing their part in code breaking heroism, however, crosswords have also been suspected of having been used in the service of treason.

The British intelligence service MI5 had its suspicions when, on August 17, 1942, the word DIEPPE appeared as an answer in the *Telegraph* puzzle and two days later there was a calamitous raid on the Channel port of that name. The intelligence officer Lord Tweedsmuir, son of spy novelist John Buchan, conducted "an immediate and exhaustive inquiry" and concluded that "it was just a remarkable coincidence—a complete fluke."

A one-off could be overlooked, even in a context as close to 1940s military intelligence as the crossword. But not an eight-off.

On May 22, 1944, another *Telegraph* puzzle by the same constructor contained the clue "Red Indian on the Missouri," which yielded the answer OMAHA. The Nebraskan city was not to be subject to an Allied raid, but "Omaha" was the secret code name for the beach in Normandy where US troops were to land in a fortnight's time. This would have seemed like just another fluke . . . if it weren't for the fact that code names for other D-Day beaches—JUNO, GOLD, UTAH, and SWORD—had all appeared in the *Telegraph* puzzle in the previous months.

In the week and a half following OMAHA, *Telegraph* puzzles included the clues "This bush is a center of nursery revolutions" (MULBERRY, the code name for the operation's floating harbors), "Britannia and he hold to the same thing" (NEPTUNE, the naval-assault stage), and "— but some bigwig like this has stolen some of it at times" (OVERLORD, the name for D-Day itself).

The constructor, Leonard Dawe, received a home visit from a pair of MI5 agents. Since a copy of the Overlord plan had recently blown out of a window of military HQ at Norfolk House, MI5 was at that point extremely sensitive to leaks. "They turned me inside out," remembered Dawe, and made him burn the notebooks he used to work on clues, but they found no evidence that the crosswords were being used to convey information to the enemy.

Dawe was a headmaster as well as a constructor, and in 1984 one of his former pupils, Ronald French, spoke to *The Telegraph*. French was fourteen during the D-Day landings and said that he and the other schoolboys used to help fill the empty grids and that Dawe would later clue the words they had chosen. Why, though, did that grid filling include secret military code words? Because, insisted French, the names of the operations were well known around the school: The pupils had overheard chatter among Canadian and American soldiers posted nearby and picked up on the odd exciting and mysterious word.

Perhaps. The lives of agents—and suspected agents—are, in their ambiguities, more like clues than answers, and the schoolboy-chatter explanation is a little too neat and decidedly too cute. Sometime *Telegraph* crossword editor Val Gilbert suspects that someone will, when clearing out an attic, find something that yields more details. "I hope," she wrote, "they will contact *The Daily Telegraph* when they do."

Whatever the truth, Dawe's puzzles raised serious concerns. The War Office banned the appearance of crosswords in papers headed for the Dominions (Canada, Australia, and so on) to stem a possible security breach and, following the liberation of Paris, newspapers there were forbidden to publish crosswords. Nowadays, it is tempting to see this as an overreaction. How, after all, might Hermann Göring have used the information in *The Telegraph*'s grids? Perhaps this is best understood as a period detail, understandable paranoia among those whose every working moment was spent looking for esoteric meanings and arcane ambiguity. In the age of microtransmitters and advanced encryption algorithms, the crossword as tool of espionage now feels downright quaint.

But consider Dr. Sawsan Alhaddad, the Cleveland anesthesiologist who was recruited in 2002 by the CIA as part of a plan to persuade her brother to defect from an important nuclear role in Iraq. To help her remember the details of her brief, the agency offered her a kit involving invisible ink and fast-burning paper. Too risky to carry when flying to Baghdad, Alhaddad thought.

Instead, she memorized the specifics and then wrote mnemonics into the squares of the crossword puzzles that would seem perfectly innocent in her luggage. The mission was successful: Alhaddad met her brother and brought back news—or, rather, non-news—of the lack of an Iraqi nuclear program. While her journey may have ultimately failed to avert a war, it remains at least a testament to old-fashioned, crossword-based spycraft.

(Of course, there is another type who spends his or her professional life in pursuit of clues. Just as popular in the twentieth century and even more identified with genre fiction—and boasting an even stronger affinity with the apparently humble puzzle . . .)

GUMSHOE

Crosswords and the detective novel

> *"It's all clues, isn't it? Crosswords are far more exotic and exciting than police work. Most murders don't require solving because they haven't been planned."*
>
> —INSPECTOR MORSE

The crossword took off at the same time as the whodunit and the jigsaw. It's tempting to explain the appeal of all three puzzles by some primeval urge to solve, but that type of explanation raises more questions than it answers—which may be the sign of a good puzzle but is also indicative of a bad piece of analysis. Attributing action to a "need" does no more than restate its existence.

Certainly, there's an overlap between these forms of puzzle.

Georges Perec constructed crosswords for *Le Point* newspaper and frames his experimental novel *La Vie mode d'emploi* using jigsaws; the pioneering cryptic constructor Torquemada, also a critic, reviewed 1,200 detective novels over four years; and Edgar Allan Poe, the godfather of the mystery story, concealed such elaborate messages in his poetry that some verses are practically double acrostics.

For some commentators, what all these forms of puzzle have in common is that they are a waste of time. In his epic *English History 1914–1945*, the historian A. J. P. Taylor finds a little value in detective fiction for providing "accurate social detail" for the historian of the period, then dismisses the genre as "[otherwise] without significance: an intellectual game like the crosswords, which became a universal feature in the newspapers at this time." His counterpart A. N. Wilson goes further in his book *The Victorians*:

> *The cryptic crossword and the whodunit mystery story were two distinctive products of their time, expressions no doubt of the belief that if one could only worry at a problem for long enough it would have a single simple solution: Keynesian or Marxist economic theory, Roman Catholic, communist or fascist doctrine.*

The connection sounds neat enough, but it doesn't stand up. A decent crossword is the very opposite of simplistic: Its whole appeal is based on the ambiguity of language and on the solver's skepticism about what is going on. Likewise, not all detective yarns provide the simple solutions that Wilson discerns, as can testify anyone who has tried to puzzle out who killed the chauffeur Owen Taylor in Raymond Chandler's *The Big Sleep*—including Chandler himself, who was asked that question by the team adapting his novel for the screen and had to admit ignorance.

Stephen Sondheim—unofficial US ambassador for the cryptic and himself the creator of stage whodunit *Getting Away with Murder* and coauthor of the ludic murder-mystery movie *The Last of Sheila*—saw a similar affinity, but thought this was something to be celebrated.

"A good clue," he insisted, "can give you all the pleasures of being duped that a mystery story can." Among those pleasures are apparent innocence, surprise, and the catharsis of exposing what has really been going on. Sondheim proved his point when he constructed a puzzle titled "Murder Mystery" in which the clues took the form of missing words in a miniature narrative:

> *"I suggest we step into the study, where the victim's flight from the murderer began, to 40A(3) if his desk will 44A(5) us further clues."*

The constructor as whodunit writer? Sure, why not? Both, if they wish to dodge charges of unfairness, must give all the necessary information such that the "solution" will make sense in retrospect. Both must avoid making this too obvious, and both are probably more prone to making it too arcane. Novice constructors have a tendency to write clues that make perfect sense to themselves but prove impenetrable to solvers.

Agatha Christie seemed to be talking about her own craft in

the novel *Why Didn't They Ask Evans?* when she had Lady Frances Derwent muse on a clue to a murder given by another character. "It's like making crossword puzzles," she remarks. "You write down a clue and you think it's too idiotically simple and that everyone will guess it straight off, and you're frightfully surprised when they simply can't get it in the least."

The affection has long been mutual, with mystery writers weaving fictional crossword puzzles into their plots for a century. In 1928, Dorothy L. Sayers's nobleman detective Lord Peter Wimsey begins the story "The Fascinating Problem of Uncle Meleager's Will" flouncing around in silk pajamas, his every step "a conscious act of enjoyment," helping his butler with a clue.

The plot concerns a young woman who has begun experimenting with socialism. Her late uncle had been of the firm conviction that a "woman who pretends to be serious is wasting her time and spoiling her appearance," so he resolved to teach this young woman a lesson by favoring her in his will but obscuring the contents of the document in crossword form.

It is only when Lord Peter falls into Uncle Meleager's pond—or, as Sayers has it, his impluvium—that he finds the grid on its watery square-tiled floor. The puzzle is reproduced in the story; it goes beyond cryptics in its esotericism and is not for the faint of heart. Here is a sample clue, which will be part Greek to many readers:

2.VI. "Bid 'ον και μη 'ον farewell?" Nay, in this
The sterner Roman stands by that which is.

. . . and the annotated solution Sayers provides at the end of the book with the completed grid . . .

2.VI. EST: 'ον και μη 'ον = est and non est*—the problem of being and not-being. Ref. Marlowe:* Doctor Faustus *I.1.*

Sorry? Sorry. More traditional and accessible fare is to be found in tales such as Vincent Fuller's 1925 potboiler *The Long Green Gaze: A Crossword Puzzle Mystery*, where the suspects in a poisoning case communicate with one another using crossword clues and the answers are given at the end in a sealed section. Likewise in the same year's *Crime of the Crossword* by John Garland, a trader in floor tiles is murdered and the arrangement of some of his tiles relates to a set of clues.

Since then, authors have reveled in titles along the lines of *A Six-Letter Word for Death* (Patricia Moyes, 1983) and *With This Puzzle, I Thee Kill* and *You Have the Right to Remain Puzzled* (Parnell Hall, 2003 and 2006). The best of the subgenre is Herbert Resnicow's *Murder Across and Down*, in which the killer of a crossword constructor is revealed by a series of dastardly puzzles set by the relentlessly ingenious real-life puzzler Henry Hook.

The crosswordiest tec, though, remains Inspector Morse, the creation of Colin Dexter, himself a crossword constructor. Dexter named his detective, Morse's sidekick Lewis, and many murder suspects after fellow solvers who repeatedly beat him in the monthly clue-writing competition in British Sunday paper *The Observer*.

Dexter not only made Morse a solver—one so addicted that

he puts time aside for the fearsome *Listener* puzzle (see the SONDHEIM chapter above); he also makes crossword solving a vital part of the detective's tool kit.

In the story *The Silent World of Nicholas Quinn*, Morse has been trying to establish which of the suspects in a murder case might have visited a cinema to see a pornographic film. He takes the time out to solve the London *Times*'s puzzle, taking an impressive twelve and a half minutes; he would have been within ten minutes but for the clue "In which are the Islets of Langerhans (8)," for which he has —A—C—E—S.

When the inspector twigs that the constructor is trying to make him conjure up a sea that fits those letters rather than PANCREAS, he sees that the suspects had been acting like a crossword constructor: trying to make him work out who had been in the cinema when nobody had been there at all.

(It's a reminder that solving of both the recreational type and the crime-fighting professional variety works best when it does not pick up merely on the clues that are provided—indeed, it is most satisfying and rewarding when what appears to be a clue is in fact a red herring. Identifying what you are not being told, deducing what you are being induced—misleadingly—to infer. An invaluable side effect of solving and certainly, very far from simplistic. Whodunits have provided some of the most ingenious crosswords in the first hundred years of the puzzle. The puzzle that should be remembered as the best of all likewise appeared in fictional form—but this one was not in a mystery story; neither was it *wholly* fictional . . .)

SIMPSON

The most audacious feat of multimedia crosswording

The best single puzzle from the first century of the crossword was published in the Sunday edition of *The New York Times* on November 16, 2008. It has more than a passing connection with the episode of *The Simpsons* that was broadcast that night—"Homer and Lisa Exchange Cross Words"—and the story starts the previous spring.

One of the writer-producers from the *Simpsons* team attended a talk at University of California, Los Angeles in May 2007. The speaker was *New York Times* crossword editor Will Shortz and came in the wake of the documentary *Wordplay*, in which we get an affecting glimpse of the intense world of crossword tournaments (see the chapter FAST above).

Simpsons supremo James L. Brooks was inspired by these

scenes and decided to afflict Lisa with a love of wordplay and send her to a "Citywide Crossword Tournament"—hence the meeting that followed the UCLA talk, at which it was agreed that Shortz would help out with the story of Lisa's new hobby and make a cameo appearance. That was nowhere close to the ambition realized in the broadcast episode, but for the time being, it was an excellent fit.

(It should also be noted that *The Simpsons* has contributed handsomely to the English language: Homer's annoyed grunt is a more satisfying sense of DOH than "Fiber of the gomuti palm," as those three letters were clued in the first-ever crossword; MEH is a splendid way of expressing indifference; and until the line of dialogue "it's a perfectly cromulent word," English had been lacking a facetious way of insisting that something is legitimate in order to convey that it isn't.)

In the story, an irrepressible Lisa becomes a crossword convert. Her school superintendent finds her making crossing words out of the playground's hopscotch squares—a compulsion to see puzzles where none exist that is familiar to solvers old and young—and he inspires her to enter a puzzle tournament. Naturally, she reaches the final.

Homer, gambling in a nearby bar, bets against her, and when Lisa discovers his treachery, we witness some heartbreaking scenes: Homer is at a loss for how to make it up to his daughter, and a distraught Lisa gives up on solving altogether. Toward the end of the episode, Marge suggests that the *New York Times* puzzle might be a cheering way for Lisa to spend a couple of hours.

Lisa's fire is reignited: "A couple of hours?! I can do the Sunday puzzle in less than one hour. 'Couple of hours'!"—and on completing that day's puzzle in record time, she notices something unusual hidden in the main diagonal: DUMBDADSORRY-FORHISBET.

Yes, a chastened Homer has persuaded Will Shortz to publish a puzzle with an apology in the form of a secret message. That might seem like a fanciful piece of fiction, but as we saw in the chapter NINA above, advanced-level constructors are prone to using the diagonals or perimeters of their puzzles to conceal secret messages.

Yet there's another reason why DUMBDADSORRYFOR-HISBET is not unrealistic: It was real. That is, the puzzle that Lisa solves was an actual puzzle, printed in the edition of the real-world *New York Times* that was published on the day of the episode's first broadcast.

This is where Will Shortz went one better than the *Simpsons* team's ambitions. He had commissioned Merl Reagle, one of the *NYT*'s most playful and imaginative constructors, to construct the grid. Three decades before, Reagle had gone to an alternative weekly called the *Los Angeles Reader* and suggested that they publish some puzzles he'd been compiling. As he approached the building, he was hoping to meet the paper's cartoonist, the then little-known Matt Groening, who of course went on to create *The Simpsons*. He discovered that he had just passed him on the way in. Talking to the *Times*'s crossword blog in 2008, he ruefully recalled:

> *If I had arrived just 15 seconds sooner I would've had the chance to meet him and tell him how much I liked his*

comic and I've always imagined that we would've been at least casual friends from that day on. I can't tell you how often I've thought about those 15 seconds.

In 2008 Reagle made up for this missed opportunity in spades, designing all the puzzles featured in "Homer and Lisa Exchange Cross Words"—including those Lisa makes from the hopscotch squares. Even though none of the grids appears for long, Reagle was insistent that any solvers among the viewers should feel that the show had taken the trouble to get the crosswords right.

This attention to detail is sadly lacking in most television crossword props. Devoted solvers get used to having the illusion of reality punctured by glimpses of asymmetrical grids or implausible clueing devices, even in programs and films where the attention to detail is otherwise impeccable. Pity the ardent crossworder when he or she beholds in unbelieving horror the complete absence of 1 acrosses or 1 downs in the puzzles containing apparent kill orders in espionage series *Rubicon*, or the action-comedy movie *Hot Fuzz*, in which the puzzle tackled by Billie Whitelaw's hotelier has a jaw-dropping 59 percent proportion of black squares.

If you want to avoid a subset of your audience drifting off, harrumphing, "Since when did a national newspaper allow two-letter entries?," the lesson is a clear one. If you need a fictional crossword, tell your props master or mistress to subcontract the work to a constructor. Any constraint the script might put on them is just the kind of challenge they like, and for no other reason than that they can work within it. At one point in "Homer and Lisa Exchange Cross Words," Lisa's tournament rival announces: "I think I'll warm up with a bunch of Qs," and dots his competition grid with them. It's a gag, but Reagle constructed a workable grid with Qs exactly where the animators had arbitrarily thrown them.

As for the final puzzle, everyone involved was aware that the reveal would be incredible for any viewers who had solved that day's *New York Times* puzzle. There is the odd *Simpsons* reference—MAGGIE hidden in TEXASA&MAGGIES, for example, but nothing that would arouse suspicions of conspiracy. Unless, that is, you're so familiar with the show's theme tune that you noticed that the other diagonal contained the letters:

F A B D C A F D B B B C B B B C E F F F F

These are the final twenty-one notes of the melody; the E is in fact an E-flat, but Reagle had of course made sure that the answer containing the E was, well, EFLAT. Otherwise, the plan was that solvers should work on what they believed was a completely normal Sunday puzzle, then see yellow animated fingers working on the same grid that same evening.

Even in the unlikely event that anyone spotted that message in the diagonal, DUMBDADSORRYFORHISBET, it would have meant nothing to anyone who hadn't been working on the show. One of the greatest pleasures in themed puzzles is what crossworders call the "penny-drop moment," but never before or since has the pleasure been as delayed or as gratifying as watching Lisa mutter some clues you'd solved that morning before realizing that the denouement of the episode has been hiding in plain view.

There is a good overlap between those who solve the *NYT* on Sundays and *Simpsons* viewers, and minds were undoubtedly fried. *New York* magazine's Nitsuh Abebe was solving while he watched, and says, "There was this slow and uncanny real-time convergence between the two." He began to wonder if he was "just imagining arcane connections between television and reality," and the moment of revelation was "like being Bruce Willis at the end of *The Sixth Sense*."

And that was not all. The fictional Reagle adds that Homer also asked him to include an implausibly demanding acrostic relating to a subplot in which Lisa decides to change her surname from Simpson to Marge's maiden name, Bouvier. So the first letters of the clues read, in order: DEAR LISA YOU MAKE ME SO HAPPY REALLY REALLY REALLY HAPPY SORRY HE TOLD ME I NEEDED A HUNDRED FORTY FOUR LETTERS WHAT WAS MY POINT AGAIN OH RIGHT BOUVIER OR SIMPSON I CHERISH YOU.

This idea for the acrostic came from the real-world Reagle; while he might have regretted it when the scriptwriters sent back a message that meant so many clues had to begin with the letter Y, the worlds of crosswords and television would be so much poorer without this remarkable feat of construction.

(There are other ways of scrambling solvers' minds, of course—not all of them as welcome . . .)

CREEPY-CRAWLY—OR WHAT IT IS LIKELY TO DO?

BUG

How to vex, rile, gall, or miff the solver

Here are some clues from the crossword in the *National Enquirer* . . .

> *"Five-headed cow born in Vermont"*
> *"State with the most UFO babies"*
> *"Aphrodisiac found in every kitchen cabinet"*
> *"Where Franco's brain is being kept alive"*

—according, that is, to the sitcom *Cheers*. The answers are MAYBELLE, ARKANSAS, OREGANO, and FISHTANK—dubious to you perhaps, but perfectly sound in the opinion of dedicated solver Carla Tortelli.

Margaret Farrar, the mother of the modern crossword, recalled a letter she had received from an eight-year-old boy who saw that while WOODENLEG would fit the squares in a puzzle she had edited, the answer should be IVORYLEG—since the leg in question was Captain Ahab's and he had read the book. "Perfectly true," she reflected, "but I couldn't help wondering, rather testily, what an eight-year-old was doing reading *Moby-Dick*."

Since the creators of crosswords are in the business of testing solvers on what they do or do not know, it is quite understandable that some of those solvers relish the opportunity to tell the teacher that his or her facts are wrong. "Frogs hop, Sir," one correspondent informed Will Shortz politely but firmly, "but toads do not. They waddle."

Solvers are, of course, supposed to be frustrated, but only in certain ways. The best fictional depiction of the wrong way comes in the very first episode of *The West Wing*. Our introduction to White House Chief of Staff Leo McGarry is an exasperated phone call he makes to the crossword editor of *The New York Times* about 17 across. "Khaddafi," he insists, "is spelled with an H and two Ds, and isn't a seven-letter word for anything."

Leo claims to be just an everyday solver, but lets slip that he should know the correct spelling of the name of the Libyan leader because he has proposed a "preemptive Exocet missile attack against his air force."

It's a cracking subplot, but of course there is no "right" way of spelling—or rather transliterating—the name of the former Libyan leader whose name was made of a *qaf*, two *dhals*, a *fa*, and a *yaa*; more to the point, the clue would not have appeared in this way. Real-life *New York Times* puzzle editor Will Shortz told me that while the spelling in clues follows *New York Times* house style—in this case "Col. Muammar el-Qaddafi"—the answer grids are different, where, he wrote in an e-mail:

> *. . . any legitimate spelling is fair game. So in a crossword clue, I would always use "Qaddafi." In a grid, GADDAFI would be acceptable (although the clue would probably include the tag "var." in fairness to solvers).*

Puzzles also need to ensure they are not being too hard—or too easy—depending on which day of the week it is. Nothing too taxing on a Monday, please—we're just getting going, and besides, there are beginners here. But don't you dare patronize me on a Sunday, when I've put some time aside and expect a full workout. (In 1985, *The Guardian* received a letter from a solver unhappy at the "smart-arse, egg-head stunt" of printing themed puzzles on a weekday: "Number 17,164 introduces a Disney connection—on a Tuesday! Play the game, sir.")

Gauging the difficulty of a puzzle is not as simple as it might appear—ponder for a while whether you can guess what proportion of the population has access to any given item from the sum of human knowledge, and you may find that you regard puzzle editors with an increased respect, or perhaps pity.

Even stickier is the question of what solvers will find acceptable when it comes to good taste.

When Denise Sutherland's book *Solving Cryptic Crosswords For Dummies* was being prepared for the American market, the relatively innocuous clues "Five engaged in awkward caresses lead to rifts (9)" and "Jenny and I go, mischievously loving (8)" were changed to "Eve's ugly scars cause rifts (9)" and "Appreciating Jenny, I go nuts (8)." (The answers in each case are CREVASSES and ENJOYING.)

The American puzzle, it seems, is not a place for too much raunch. Even the puzzle that is in its proper place has to tread carefully. Margaret Farrar told the sixteen-year-old would-be constructor Merl Reagle that "crosswords are entertainment," advising him to avoid "things like death, disease, war and taxes—the subway solver gets enough of that in the rest of the paper."

She might well have added to that list bodily functions. In 2006, *The New York Times* had a clue that read:

Scoundrel

Seven letters, and the answer is SCUMBAG. No problem. Except that it was a big problem, and there were complaints from members of the newspaper staff as well as from readers. It's not a pleasant way to describe someone, but P. G. Wodehouse (of whom more below) had a character describe millionaires as "the scum of the earth" and he's a respectable writer, so how was offense caused?

The issue was a different, more physical, sense of "scum," and the original sense of "scumbag": a condom. For that reason, *The New York Times* tends not to use the word: When Congressman Dan Burton said of Bill Clinton, "The guy's a scumbag," the paper reported the "use of a vulgarity for a condom to describe the President." The style guide acknowledges that "taking a stand for civility in public discourse" is "sometimes at an acknowledged cost in the vividness of an article or two."

There's also a potential cost in representativeness, if the representative in question meant only that he considered the president a "base, despicable person" (as the Oxford dictionary gives the later sense) and not akin to a prophylactic.

To British solvers, this decorum is bewildering. Just as an apparently prim dowager or tweed-clad don might, in the UK, utter a profanity that would appall a stevedore, so can the apparently erudite British cryptic embrace almost all of language, including the scaggy, scuzzy, scummy bits. "Further issues might arise if this billet were not to be occupied" is a typically allusive description of a condom from the generally austere *Daily Telegraph*.

It gets worse. Merl Reagle, heeding Farrar's advice, has spoken longingly of the words that good taste precludes. "URINE would bail me out of a corner a million times a year," he lamented. "Same with ENEMA. ENEMA: talk about great letters."

But in Britain? Oh yes. One of the most distinctive UK puzzles is in the magazine *Private Eye*, a mixture of investigations and satire. Its first crossword constructor was Tiresias, better known as the parliamentarian and security service asset Tom Driberg. The magazine's official history describes his stint from 1969 until 1976 as "legendarily filthy." Driberg had been receiving a retainer for providing parliamentary gossip; when this dried up because he was not in the Commons often enough to pick up much intelligence, he suggested that he instead set a prize crossword. His biographer Francis Wheen writes:

> *Perhaps his finest moment was Crossword 98, in 1972, which had such clues as "Seamen mop up anal infusions*

(6)" (ENEMAS) and "Sounds as if you must look behind for this personal lubricant (5)" (SEBUM).

Crossword 98 offered a prize of £2, which was claimed by a Mrs. Rosalind Runcie, whose husband was then bishop of St. Albans and went on to become the archbishop of Canterbury. Those clues, you might say, rather rub the solver's face in the filth of the constructor; more frequently spotted is the clue that appears to be racy but of which the constructor can, with a straight face, insist perfect innocence. Here's one from the London *Times* Crossword Championship:

In which three couples get together for sex (5)

Well, three couples equals three times two. That's six, and the only context in which "six" is "sex" is the answer: LATIN. On other matters, both sides of the Atlantic are in general agreement.

In December 2012, if you asked any cryptic addict for the name of the best-loved constructor, the answer would almost certainly be Araucaria (see the chapter CRYPTIC above). In a 2008 interview, the retired churchman recalled the advice given to him some decades earlier by the puzzle editor of the Manchester and London *Guardian*.

"No diseases, no religion and no Bible" was the beginning, and the list ended, "No brand names and not too much by the way of politics."

Many of these sensibilities have since gone by the wayside: HOOVER is as likely to appear as a brand name as it is a politician, but the steer on diseases, at least serious ones, is generally heeded. Which made it all the more shocking when Araucaria himself published a puzzle in 2013 with a preamble that began with the news that the constructor had "18 down of the 19." Eighteen down was easy enough:

Sign of growth (6)

The solver, expecting nothing unusual, runs through the six-letter signs of the zodiac to find one that can also be indicated by "growth." Not PISCES, TAURUS, or GEMINI . . . but CANCER fits. And then, before even writing in the answer, the penny drops and the stomach lurches, with no way back: Araucaria has CANCER. Postsolve, the puzzle's preamble could be fully decoded as follows:

> *I have CANCER of the ESOPHAGUS; no CHEMOTHERAPY, just PALLIATIVE CARE; no NARCOTIC or STENT or MACMILLAN NURSE yet—plenty of MERRIMENT, though I wouldn't have chosen the timing.*

Nobody would chastise John Graham for defying the expectation that solving won't make you feel queasy: Unusually for an Araucaria, the experience wasn't in the least fun, though there was surely pleasure in marveling at the enormous chutzpah of responding to such a diagnosis with a themed puzzle. Araucaria died a month before the centenary of the crossword, and among the many obituaries and eulogies, none failed to mention with approval "18 down of the 19." In crosswords, all rules are eventually broken, and broken well.

(And for a portrait in miniature of cruciverbal frustration, let's look at one particular—very passionate and opinionated—solver . . .)

HIGHLY DESIRABLE FRUIT?

PLUM

How P. G. Wodehouse fell in and out of love with crosswords

P. G. Wodehouse knew his crosswords. We see that in his novel *Summer Moonshine*: Lady Abbott, shoeless on the settee, regretfully rejects IRVINGBERLIN as a nine-letter answer for an Italian composer beginning with a P "because, despite his other merits, too numerous to mention here, he had twelve letters, began with an *i*, and was not an Italian composer."

Her technique is familiar to any solver who has tried, against all the evidence provided by grid, clues, and crossing letters, to make a possible answer work. Luckily for Lady Abbott, her husband soon bursts in, scans the newspaper, and . . .

> *[bringing] to the problem the full force of his intellect, he took the pencil and in a firm hand wrote down the word*

> *"Pagliacci." Each helping each, was the way Sir Buckstone looked at it.*

Never mind that PAGLIACCI is an opera, not a composer: This is a touching and true portrayal of the dual solve, husband and wife complementing each other in pursuit of a filled grid.

It's no surprise that Plum, as Wodehouse is fondly known, adored crosswords—like his stories, they consist of language pared down to an elegant minimum and assembled, jigsaw-like, to a symmetric whole, all to no higher purpose than whiling away some time and raising a few smiles.

It's a pity that Wodehouse never constructed a whole puzzle, but his stories abound in clues—and in real life, Wodehouse was, at least initially, no slouch as a solver. "When he got *The* [London] *Times*," his grandson recalled, "he could do the crossword instantly, filling the answers in as if he was writing a letter." But the crosswords Wodehouse preferred were the early puzzles, which consisted purely of definitions, rather than the more elaborate wordplay that was to emerge in Britain in the early thirties.

In the twenties, when crosswords first took off, Wodehouse was living in the country of their creation. He later recalled a conversation about America and how "they're getting pretty nutty in this adopted land of mine," citing novelties such as loudspeakers on golf courses and commenting that:

> *The crossword puzzle craze is now at such a pitch, my paper informs me, that a Pittsburgh pastor is handing out crossword slips which, when solved, give the text of his sermon. They're all loony.*

Soon, however, Wodehouse was himself going nutty for crosswords. It may seem strange now, when crosswords are an unremarkable part of everyday life, but when the puzzles first appeared in fiction, they were a seriously contemporary detail. Wodehouse first mentions them, in passing, in *The Strand Magazine* in 1925. In the story "High Stakes" Bradbury Fisher annoys his rival J. Gladstone Bott by getting a place on the crossword team of Sing-Sing prison—which also boasts such nonpenitential activities as a glee club and a baseball nine.

Soon enough, Wodehouse begins to use them to inform the plot. In 1926's "The Truth About George," nervous, stammering George Mulliner is always looking in at the vicarage to ask the lovely Susan Blake for help with crosswords . . .

> *and Susan was just as constant a caller at George's cozy little cottage—being frequently stumped, as girls will be, by words of eight letters signifying "largely used in the manufacture of poppet-valves."*

Wodehouse is providing gentle observational humor about the specialist terminology demanded of solvers, but it's also a plot device to bring together two shy individuals. It is not until Susan helps George "out of a tight place with the word 'disestablishmentarianism'" that he realizes she is "precious, beloved, darling, much-loved, highly esteemed or valued" to him. The crossword as Cupid, and a happy corrective to *Brief Encounter* (see the chapter ADDICTION).

By the thirties, the craze was less fervid, and crosswords were as commonplace and contemporary as Wodehouse's slang.

Puzzles became not merely something for his characters to do but also a way to tell us a little of their personalities. Take George's first cousin once removed, Mervyn Mulliner in *Hot Water*. When he is at a loss for the name of a large Australian bird beginning with E and ending with U, he "places the matter in the hands of the editor of the Encyclopædia Britannica."

Mervyn's habit of delegating later lands him in the hot water that gives the novel its title in a subplot involving out-of-season strawberries (of course). Meanwhile, in *The Code of the Woosters*, Madeline Bassett in a moment of apparent inspiration looks at Bertie "like someone who has just solved the crossword puzzle with a shrewd 'Emu' in the top right-hand corner." Crossword emus make many appearances in Wodehouse stories; indeed, part of the pleasure of early crosswords and Wodehouse stories is the variation on familiar subjects: in crosswords, those "crosswordese" words that occur time and again; in Wodehouse, aunts, wagers, and engagements.

The thirties are the golden age for crosswords in Wodehouse. The puzzles had started appearing in all newspapers, and the cryptic form was in bloom. Wodehouse tried to keep up—indeed, in his letters, he seems more interested in the puzzle than in the news part of the newspaper, and was even prompted to join a lively debate on the London *Times*'s letters pages about one of them.

On August 17, 1934, the member of parliament Austen Chamberlain wrote to boast of finishing that paper's puzzle in forty-one minutes, adding that the provost of Eton College "measures the time required for boiling his breakfast egg by that needed for the solution of your daily crossword—and he hates a hard-boiled egg."

The implausible speed of that provost—better known today as the ghost story writer M. R. James—galled Wodehouse, who wrote his own letter five days later to convey the pleasurable frustration felt by solvers then and since. The solving times were, he protested, "g. and wormwood" to the "humble strivers" who had yet to finish a *Times* puzzle.

> *In conclusion, may I commend your public spirit in putting the good old emu back into circulation again as you did a few days ago? We of the* canaille, *now that the Sun-God Ra has apparently retired from active work, are intensely grateful for an occasional emu.*

"Canaille," by the way, means the "vile herd"—it's a self-consciously French way of referring to the lower orders, which pretty much collapses if you try to use it to describe yourself. More crosswordese? You can't deny it has its eminent fans.

By common consent, greater problems than "*beating his head against the wall for twenty minutes over a single anagram*" awaited Wodehouse as the thirties turned into the forties. The start of the Second World War found the author in Le Touquet in France, and he spent much of the early forties in internment camps, and then in Berlin, where he made some radio broadcasts to reassure his fans that he was alive and well.

The decision to broadcast on Nazi shortwave radio was not popular, however, and was regarded in England and America as at worst treasonous and at best what Bertie Wooster's Aunt Dahlia would describe as the action of a congenital idiot who "wants a nurse to lead him by the hand and some strong attendant to kick him regularly at intervals of a quarter of an hour."

His wartime letters reveal a Wodehouse anxious less about world affairs than about how the Dulwich College cricket team is faring and how soon after publication he's able to get *The Times*. "I have been able to resume my *Times* crossword puzzles," he writes to the novelist Denis Mackail in February 1945. "What is 'Exclaim when the twine gives out' in ten letters?" (This is a clue for the musical instruction STRINGEDO, and one of the most baffling, dismaying efforts at wordplay I have ever encountered.)

But even crosswords are offering less comfort as the war goes on. By May, he writes:

> *I have finally and definitely given up the* Times *crossword puzzles. The humiliation of only being able to fill in about three words each day was too much for me. I am hoping that what has happened is that they have got much more difficult, but I have a gloomy feeling that it is my brain that has gone back.*

Given up? He had. It wasn't the same in the post-war stories. No more firm hands writing PAGLIACCI, no poppet-valves acting as Valentines. Aunts lick their pencils in vain frustration, and in "Sticky Wicket at Blandings" Gally Threepwood lights a cigar and looks at *The Times* but finds that "these crossword puzzles had become so abstruse nowadays and he was basically a Sun-god-Ra and Large-Australian-bird-emu man." For a while, a butler can be relied upon to shimmy into view and solve the more challenging clues, but in 1957's *Something Fishy*, the clues are left unanswered. From an author whose stock in trade is the relief of tensions and solving of mysteries, the effect is eerie—and the experience, as when you can't finish a real-world crossword, unusually frustrating.

(Not all of crosswords' more notable devotees are quite so critical . . .)

A REGISTER OF PEOPLE—OR *THE* REGISTER OF *THE* PEOPLE?

A-LIST

Some of the more well-known among the puzzle's devotees

Any list of notable solvers is by definition partial and far from impartial. Were I, though, to assemble an All-Star Crossword Team of solvers past and present, I would choose:

Frank Sinatra, who wrote a fan letter to the *New York Times* puzzle editor giving his solving times, remarking: "What a wonderful way to pass the time and also learn new answers every day"

Christopher Robin, who would cosolve at the age of eighteen on the sofa with his father, A. A. Milne

Indira Gandhi, whose participation in a bilateral economic cooperation agreement is attributed by diplomat and champion solver Roy Dean to an ice-breaking conversation about crosswords beforehand

Norman Mailer, who told *Newsweek* in 2003 that "this is how I comb my brain every morning," adding, "I'm hurt that I'm never in one of them. And I've got a last name with three vowels. You'd think I'd be hot cakes, but I'm not"

Thomas Keneally, who, when the BBC asked what single item he would take to a desert island, chose a collection of puzzles from the London *Times*

Queen Elizabeth II, who, in a 1992 profile in *Vanity Fair*, begins each morning with the *Telegraph* crossword accompanied by kippers or kidneys on toast . . .

. . . her sister, **Princess Margaret**, who once won a book as a prize in the *Country Life* crossword competition . . .

. . . and their father, **King George VI**, whose last act before dying of a heart attack in his sleep was a late-evening crossword solve.

(Who would be on yours? You can't have Ol' Clue Eyes—I've nabbed him . . .)

TOMORROW MAKES YOU TENSE?

FUTURE

What will the crossword of the twenty-first century look like?

We have declared that the first crossword was printed on December 21, 1913, in the New York *World* newspaper. Arthur Wynne's "Word-Cross" was the rudimentary grid-plus-clues, definitions-lead-to-answers puzzle from which all others—Swedish and Japanese, straight and cryptic—have developed.

But is that definitely, indubitably true? The years following the American Civil War saw a flourishing of periodicals for veterans, keeping alive the camaraderie of the Union and Confederacy groupings, sprinkling in some reportage . . . and the odd puzzle.

The Neighbor's Home Mail described itself as the "most intensely interesting Soldier paper published in this or any other country." Also part temperance journal, the *Mail* urged former Union soldiers to subscribe in order to preserve "the little incidents and precious memories which fill the bosom of every honored veteran," adding, "Every Soldier should write jokes for it!"

In the edition for October 1874, the section of puzzles headed ENIGMATICAL PROPOSITIONS contained this challenge:

11. ***Crossword.*****—My first is in morn, but not in night; Second in wrong, but not in right; Third in over, but not in beneath; Fourth in long, but not in brief; Fifth in iron, but not in lead: Sixth in tongue but not in head; Seventh in running, but not in fleet; Whole, in awaking, we all gladly greet. BEN E. DICTION.**

☞ Who will be the first to report the solution of all the above puzzles? Who?

Is this crossword a crossword? Well, yes and no. Surely, goes the case for yes, a puzzle called a crossword that asks the solver to manipulate interlocking words is a crossword puzzle. But, counters the case for no, where is the grid? Ah, remarks the yes, but Arthur Wynne's grid was different from those we see today. It was a diamond rather than a square, and had a strange system of numbering the clues, proving that a crossword can look quite unlike today's puzzles and still count as a crossword . . .

To answer this question is not merely to split hairs; it helps us understand what the future of the crossword might be.

The chief current method of distributing a puzzle is to squish a bunch of trees until they become thin sheets of paper, then spray them with ink derived from soy juice in the shape of a grid and clues, and surround them with all manner of investigations, opinions, and advertisements. Good luck persuading a deep-pocketed entrepreneur of the sustainability of that business model.

In 1874 periodicals crammed the maximum content into the paper available, setting the type small and close together, and the nineteenth-century solver completed the puzzles on a separate sheet or in his or her head. By 1913, there was more space and more scope for diagrams, pictures . . . and grids.

The Neighbor's Home Mail "crossword" and Wynne's diamond each took a form appropriate to the workable technology of the day. As the lead blocks of hot metal gave way to digital type, the number of possible grids expanded. Crosswords have shifted with technology, and they're about to do so again.

We can understand the crossword in its current form as a result not just of the brains of the pioneering constructors but also of the possibilities of World War I–era printing.

As such, the crossword comes with a set of loose assumptions that are entirely dependent on its physical form. If a crossword comes into your consciousness by means of a newspaper, it means that certain things are expected of you, the solver:

- you will need to furnish yourself with extra kit, i.e., pencil or pen
- said crossword will be two-dimensional
- you will be expected to complete or abandon said crossword on the day of its publication, in order to make "room" for the next one
- you need not by default time the solve; the constructor cannot directly invite solvers to go into competition with one another

- the constructor must use the printed word, always in black, as the basis for clues and answers

None of these, in terms of crossword pleasure, is a shortcoming, but they all begin to seem a little arbitrary when you consider what's happened to the medium the puzzle originated in. The decline in print readership is not going away. This is explainable in part by the fact that there's nothing about a newspaper's content that demands physical form—except perhaps the crossword in its current form: the final reason for newsprint to be printed. In newsrooms and editors' offices, crosswords are considered important for loyalty and newsstand sales. This is largely based on anecdote and hunch, so I decided to commission some research to see what the numbers look like in the UK.

I discovered that around three in ten British adults attempt a crossword at least once a week, and that of solvers as a whole (72 percent solve at least occasionally), one in five says that his or her choice of newspaper has been influenced by its crossword. Newspaper proprietors might want to consider whether it's the puzzle page that is keeping physical sales from falling to zero, and constructors might feel emboldened to ask for a long-overdue pay raise.

However, even taking the most positive interpretation—that crosswords are the only remaining reason for buying a physical copy of a newspaper—the crossword approached its centenary year treading water rather than powering forward in a butterfly.

Crossworders, both constructors and solvers, might benefit from their puzzle of choice switching to another paper medium, or ponder how the experience of a puzzle with the same grid and clues might change its form in different mediums: newsprint, online (on-screen or printed out), and apps for smartphones and tablets.

On paper, the crossword is a physical activity, albeit not one that is likely to make practitioners break into a sweat. For some, the pleasure is tactile.

Orlando—a staggeringly prolific constructor who has been in the business since 1975—created a crossword site in the early days of the World Wide Web; in 2012 he reflected that online solvers seem to prefer to see on-screen something very like what they see on paper. "There's no demand for the bells and whistles," he noted—those potential bells and whistles including "hyperlinks, sound, pictures, video, and so on." Just use your imagination . . .

For those solvers accustomed by school to completing exercises by making marks on paper, who knows, there may remain in the future a vestigial two-dimensional form of the crossword. If the experience of home printing ever becomes less horrific than it is now, he or she may be printing off a daily puzzle rather than buying it from a kiosk, surrounded by all that other bumf.

One vision of this future comes from the London technology company Berg Cloud, which has produced a small home printer that automatically and inklessly produces, each morning and on thermal paper, something that is a little like a newspaper, but not quite, the aim being to reduce the cost and bother of choosing material and running it through a conventional printer. Users choose from features such as news, to-do lists, and puzzles for consumption on the bus or train, for example: The available items include sudokus and a super-quick version of the London *Times* crossword that contains one across and one down clue (super-quick, that is, assuming that they are the right two clues for your mood on a given weekday).

After the initial setup of the Berg Cloud printer, the puzzles are simply there, every day, just like they are in the newspapers. Indeed, the past propagation of puzzles is explained in part by their presence in a paper. The crossword might not be your destination when you buy a paper—and, typically, it doesn't have anything to do with news—but a sufficiently long journey or a day with sufficiently grim reports might divert you to the crossword page: the only part of a paper that offers instant interactivity. The potential new solver is buying a crossword without realizing that he or she is doing so. But as newspapers become sprawling websites, some with a separate price package for the puzzles, the cost of entry rises.

Even for the seasoned and paid-up solver, the digital crossword is in danger of getting lost. On a smartphone or tablet, every other format of entertainment and communication is converging to jostle for the limited attention of the user of a single device—and most of the other "gaming" options are germane to their form, asking to be swiped, tilted, stroked, and tapped in new and gratifying ways: the touch screen equivalents of Orlando's "bells and whistles."

Such things are not alien to the crossword: As early as 1982 the American cryptic evangelist Henry Hook, whose career was described in *The New Yorker* as "one long effort to subvert our safe assumptions about puzzles, to make them as unsettling and unpredictable as art," showcased another approach. It was a puzzle called "Sound Thinking," in which many of the clues were announced over a loudspeaker, his contribution to the 1982 US Open Crossword Puzzle Championship, and a perfect ten of context plus content.

The challenge for crossword constructors and editors is to make wordplay work in the devices that are replacing print. New types of clue, using nonverbal hints, seem certain to emerge: Some may become part of the standard armory; some will branch off to make new kinds of puzzles, using colors, sounds, and shapes, which may or may not be called "crosswords."

So far, most of the features publishers have added to crosswords have been along the same lines as those that adorn news: shareability and other social accessories such as leaderboards for the speediest solvers (see the chapter FAST above). But crosswords are not like news; they're not made up of facts but are abstract edifices in which words are spelled out in unconventional directions. Those directions currently number two—across and down—but more are possible.

One possible direction of travel is suggested by another look at *The Neighbor's Home Mail* and the puzzle in its twentieth-century incarnation. The 1874 "crossword" could be re-presented as a straight line of cells into which the solver writes the word MORNING: essentially a single across entry. For newsprint crosswords, the "grid" metaphor expands the area of play to a plane. Now screens can take their users in more than two dimensions, and metaphors other than a grid or a plane may explode into view while the crossword remains recognizable as a crossword.

The constructor Eric Westbrook is a teacher; he is also le-gally blind. For him, there is nothing inevitable about limiting the directions of clues to across and down, and he has quietly shown an amazing way of subtly rethinking the crossword.

When Westbrook constructs a puzzle, the analogy he uses is an apartment block. Each square becomes a room, and the words may be spelled out in front of you, to your right, or down through the stories beneath your feet. While the crossword is more engrossing, solving it does not, as you might suspect, take a lot of getting used to: The solver soon forgets that there's anything out of the ordinary going on and engages with the clues and entries.

As Eric points out, most solvers could walk through their own homes blindfolded. "I walk around three-dimensional grids until I know them inside out and all the letters are in their places. It's not quick—but it's certainly easier than doing a school timetable." Here is a partially filled grid in which, if you adjust your eyes to reading in different directions, you can see the answers starting from square one, CHARING operating as an across, CHALK as a regular down (now going away from the solver) and CROSS reading (down) down.

Currently, Eric's puzzles exist in a two-dimensional medium. Having filled his grids, he recruits established constructors to set the clues and prints the puzzles as calendars to raise money for children's charities. He is certainly a maverick, but that doesn't mean he's completely out on his own: There are others, too, building in a third dimension. The *Listener* puzzle series (see the chapter SONDHEIM above) may be printed on the flat pages of the London *Times*, but it has asked its solvers to cut out its grids and restructure them in the form of a Rubik's Cube, the one-sided loop known as a Möbius strip, and even the abstract

single-surfaced Klein bottle. If any puzzle embraces time as the fourth dimension—a grid in which the correct letters depend on what day it is, say—it will surely be *The Listener*.

Another exciting new direction was suggested by Tracy

Gray in a *New York Times* puzzle based on the "right turn on red" traffic instruction. In its down clues, if the solver encountered the letters RED, he or she changed direction, so, for example, INSHREDS, CLAIREDANES, and CHEEREDON become:

I	*C*		*C*
N	*L*		*H*
S	*A*		*E*
H	*I*		*E*
REDS	*REDANES*	*and*	*REDON*

Deviating from across and down does not mean that these crosswords are not crosswords. It merely suggests that, just as words can currently inhabit spaces above and below one another, the puzzles of the future may place them in front of and behind one another. Which is not really so big a change, is it?

(So, while the crossword remains a physical activity, let us say good-bye to its newsprint form with a pseudoscientific investigation into what your choice of writing device reveals about you . . .)

IMPLEMENT

Your character as revealed by how you complete a puzzle

Pen: You prefer deductive reasoning. You expect ambiguity to resolve itself and to remain resolved. You know that each entry in the grid is waiting for one and only one word, and you withhold judgment until you are sure which one word that is. Then you can look at the crossing answers safe in the knowledge that the letters entered are correct. For you, the basic unit of information in a puzzle is The Clue. You may come unstuck, however, when The Clue equally suggests two answers and only the crossing letters reveal which is The Entry.

Pencil: You are one for inductive reasoning. You accept that even when something appears to be the case, you may have overlooked some key piece of information. You build your interpretation of the world and of a grid tentatively. You demand as much information as possible before you commit. For you, the most important unit of information in a puzzle is The Grid, and each answer depends on more than its clue. You may come unstuck when the space for a tricky clue is filled with lightly scrawled letters, some correct and some incorrect.

Wax crayon: You are desperate to solve, traveling with no writing implements other than something of your child's (now fourteen) that you have inexplicably found in a pocket. You will come unstuck when the crayon becomes so blunt that each letter fills four squares at once.

RESOURCES

The resources I found most useful and which are most recommended for further reading are:

The blogs *Fifteensquared, Times for the Times,* and *Big Dave's Crossword Blog*

of enormous use to cryptic newcomers and incidentally the only way of recovering half-remembered clues and devices

Don Manley's *Chambers Crossword Manual* (Chambers, 2001)

the best explanation of the innards of puzzles

***75 Years of the* Times *Crossword* (HarperCollins UK, 2005)**

an anniversary collection of puzzles and the reminiscences of editors, constructors, and solvers

***A Clue to Our Lives: 85 Years of the* Guardian *Cryptic Crossword* (Guardian Books, 2008)**

Sandy Balfour's stock-take of *Guardian* puzzles, constructors, and culture, and its sister volumes *Pretty Girl in Crimson Rose* (Atlantic, 2003) and *I Say Nothing* (Atlantic, 2006)

***From Square One: A Meditation, with Digressions, on Crosswords* (Scribner, 2009)**

a thoughtful, funny book by Dean Olsher that would be an excellent read whatever its subject matter

The Strange World of the Crossword
(M. & J. Hobbs, 1974)

Roger Millington's rambunctious tour through the state of crosswording at the age of sixty-odd

Georges Perec's *Les Mots croisés, procédés de considérations de l'auteur sur l'art et la manière de croiser les mots* (Mazarine, 1979)

the playful Frenchman's philosophy of puzzling

Tony Augarde's *Oxford Guide To Word Games*
(Oxford University Press, 1984)

which also has chapters on letter games, alphabet games, Scrabble . . .

***Wordplay* (2006)**

Patrick Creadon and Christine O'Malley's documentary about American puzzlers

***Timeshift: How to Solve a Cryptic Crossword* (2008)**
Georgina Harvey's BBC documentary about the UK cryptic scene

This book also draws on, inter alia, Afrit's *Armchair Crosswords: A Book for Leisure Moments* (Derek Harrison, 2009); CC Bombaugh's *Oddities and Curiosities of Words and Literature* (Dover, 1961); the Oulipo collection *La Littérature Potentielle: Créations, Re-créations, Récréations* (Gallimard, 1973); Michael Smith's *Station X: The Codebreakers of Bletchley Park* (Pan, 2003); Marcel Danesi's *The Puzzle Instinct: The Meaning of Puzzles in Human Life* (Indiana University Press, 2002); Ben Tausig's *The Curious History of the Crossword: 100 Puzzles from Then and Now* (Race Point, 2013); the 'pataphysicist Luc Etienne's *L'Art Du Contrepet* (Pauvert, 1957); Stanley Newman's *Cruciverbalism: A Crossword Fanatic's Guide to Life in the Grid* (Harper, 2006); Peter Schwed's *Turning the Pages: An Insider's Story of Simon & Schuster 1924–1984* (Macmillan, 1984); Gilbert Renault's *Le Livre Du Courage Et De La Peur* (Aux Trois Couleurs, 1945); *The New York Times* crossword blog *Wordplay*; the Jeremiah Farrell conversation with Johnny Gee at barelybad.com/xwdthemes_110596.htm; the charity calendar puzzles at calendarpuzzles.co.uk; the articles "The Riddler: Meet the Marquis de Sade of the Puzzle World" in *The New Yorker* and "A Funny Thing Happened To Stephen Sondheim" in *La Scena Musicale*, the *Inspector Morse* episode "The Settling of the Sun" and the British Diplomatic Oral History Programme.

The across answers to the telekinesis puzzle, by the way, are ERDA and EYED—and here is the solution, a century later, to Arthur Wynne's first puzzle:

> **Across** *(top to bottom): FUN; SALES; RECEIPT; MERE; FARM; DOVE; RAIL; MORE; DRAW; HARD; TIED; LION; SAND; EVENING; EVADE; ARE.* **Down** *(left to right): DOH; MORAL; REVERIE; SERE; DOVE; FACE; NEVA; RULE; NARD; NEIF; SIDE; SPAR; TANE; TRADING; MIRED; LAD.*

ACKNOWLEDGMENTS

All those with whom I learned to solve, including my brother Alexander, my late dad, Shaun Pye, Charlie Rowlands, Sean Walsh, Mark Chappell, and Lucy Brett.

The constructors who have guided me through their world including Araucaria, Rufus, Enigmatist, Quixote, Paul, Arachne, Monk, Azed, Tramp, Orlando, Puck, Shed, Brendan Emmett Quigley, Audreus, Gordius, Micawber, Goujeers, Trazom, Hot, and Philistine.

Those who have provided information and wisdom including Sean Walsh, David Bellos, Kathryn Friedlander, Noah Veltman, Anne R. Bradford, Denise Sutherland, Richard Browne, Mike Hutchinson, Peter Biddlecombe, Will Shortz, Evie Eysenburg, Nitsuh Abebe, Shuchi Upadhyay, Deb Ablem, Jane Teather, Charlotte Murray, Brendan Carr, Stephan Shakespeare, Faria Iqbal, Michael Price, Jane Sewell, Julian Mitchell, and Colin Dexter—and Eric Westbrook and Jerry Farrell for their puzzles.

From *The Guardian*: Janine Gibson, Hugh Stephenson, Kate Carter, Rachel Dixon, Pamela Hutchinson, and Rachel Holmes—and the readers of and commenters at *The Guardian Crossword Blog*.

ACKNOWLEDGMENTS

Those who enabled this book to sit in your hands: my editor Brooke Carey and agent Andrew Gordon; others from publishing including my UK editor Helen Conford, Rose Goddard, Leslie Hansen, Stefan McGrath, and Jessica Sindler.

For feeding and watering my playing with words: my English teacher Kenneth Fitzell and my mum.

For waiting: Lucy and Raphael.

INDEX

Abbreviations, 47, 101, 122
Abebe, Nitsuh, 144
Across
  book section defined, xi
  creating numbering system, 11
  origin of jargon, 20–21
Acrostics (puzzle), 7, 21–25, 32, 86, 134, 144. *See also* Mnemonics
Adams, Franklin P., 9
Addiction, crosswording as
  cheating and, 95–96
  depiction in TV and movies, 137–138
  enforcement of punishment, 15
  hold on Victorian England, 22
  impact on relationships, 109–112
  lure of cryptic crossword to, 76–78
  researching motivations, 98–99
  satisfying need for puzzles, 8
  sharing experience with others, 113–115
The Adventures of Mr. Verdant Green (Bede), 24
Afrit's Injunction, 37–39
"A Funny Thing Happened to Stephen Sondheim" (Lebrecht), 177
Age-related mental health, crosswording and, 97–102
Alhaddad, Sawsan (Dr.), 131–132
All About Steve (movie), 115
"All-over interlock," 11, 49, 80, 95, 163
Alphametic (aka cryptarithm), 12
Alzheimer's, staving off onset, x, 97–102
American Civil War, 162–164
American Crossword Puzzle Tournament
  1999 competition, 74–75
  2012 competition, 119–121
  competition stress and pressure, 103–104
  training tips, 106–108
Anagram (puzzle), 4, 25–28, 60, 79, 82–87, 114, 125, 157
Anderson, John B., 65
Antonyms, 101
Archer, Lord Jeffrey, 67, 78, 87–88
Armchair Crosswords: A Book of Leisure Moments (Ritchie), 37, 177
Armstrong, Lance, 66
Artificial intelligence, 119
Artificial language, 7, 34
The Art of the Spoonerism (Étienne), 71
Augarde, Tony, 176

Bacon, Francis, 21
Balfour, Sandy, 175–176
Bass, Jennie, 116–117
Bately, Alfred, 33–34
Beastie Boys (music group), 59

INDEX

The Beatles (music group), 3
Bede, Cuthbert, 24
Beeman, Mark, 107
Bell, Adrian, 18–19, 38
Bell, Martin, 18
Bello, David, 55
Berg Cloud, 166–167
Bernstein, Leonard, 76
Berry, Patrick, 68
The Bible, 25
Biddlecombe, Peter, 107
Big Daves's Crossword Blog, 175
The Big Sleep (Chandler), 135
Black Speech (made-up language), 34
Bombaugh, C. C., 177
Book returns, publisher practice of, 10
Borges, Jorge Luis, 55
The Boston Globe, 116–117
Bowra, Maurice, 70
Brief Encounter (movie), 109–112, 155
British Diplomatic Oral History Programme (BDOHP), 178
Brontë, Charlotte, 21
Brooksbank, Peter, 105
Brooks, James L., 139–140
Brooks, Rebekah, 31
Buchan, John (Lord Tweedsmuir), 129–130
Burton, Dan, 148

Carroll, Lewis, 36–37, 39
Carruthers, F. D., 11
Carter, Jimmy, 65
Central Intelligence Agency (CIA), 131–132
Chamberlain, Austen, 156
Chambers Crossword Manual (Manley), 44, 175
The Chambers Dictionary, 58, 78
Championships. *See* Tournaments and Championships
Chandler, Raymond, 135
Character, crosswording and, 172–173
Charade clues, 85
Cheating, rules about, 91–96
Christie, Agatha, 21, 135–136
Clerihew (poem format), 12
Clinton, William J. ("Bill"), 63–65, 67, 103–104, 148
Cloud computing, crosswording and, 166–167
Clue(s). *See also* Crossword construction
  acrostic, 7, 21–25, 32, 86, 134, 144
  anagram, 4, 25–28, 60, 79, 82–83, 86–88, 114, 125, 157
  as basic unit of crossword, 31
  charade, 85
  computer-generated puzzles, 121–124
  cryptic definition, 81–82
  deductive reasoning and, 172–173
  double definition, 80
  hidden answer, 83–84
  multiple meanings, 63–65
  origin of jargon, 20–21
  "penny-drop" moment of clarity, 98–99
  playing tricks and maintaining fairness, 36–39, 146–148
  reversal, 84–85
  role in whodunit mysteries, 134–136
  role in wordplay, 25–26
  soundalikes, 85–86
  translations into other languages, 52–55
  use of palindrome, 26–28
  use of slang, 57–60
A Clue to Our Lives (Balfour), 175–176
The Code of the Woosters (Wodehouse), 156
Colonel Rémy (Gilbert Renault), 72
Computers and digital advances. *See* Technology, crosswording and
Coward, Noël, 109
Cox, Emily, 116–117
Creadon, Patrick, 176
Cresswell, I., 77
Crime of the Crossword (Garland), 137
Crisp, Ruth ("Crispa"), 123
Crossword bots, 119–121

INDEX

Crossword construction. *See also* Clue(s); Grid
about beginning, 10, 26, 115, 162–164
adapting language differences, 49–51
basic units of crosswording, 31
beyond printed puzzles, 165–171
breaking rules of decorum and taste, 147–152
computer-generated puzzles, 121–122
creating ability to "lose gracefully," 122
creating clues, 37, 39–40, 93, 122–123
cryptic clues, 79–88
depiction in novels, 134–138
favorite English words, 45–48
getting facts wrong, 145–146
learning the art, 115
replacement of print, 165–169
staving off dementia, 102
use of spoonerisms, 73
using slang, 58–60
using the nina, 32–35, 141
Crossword constructors
about anonymity and pseudonyms, 81–82
Adrian Bell, 18–19, 38
A. F. Ritchie ("Afrit"), 37–39, 83–84
Brendan Emmett Quigley, 32, 58, 79, 114
Brian Greer, 83
Bunthorne, 86
Chifonie, 86
Colin Dexter, 137
David Moseley ("Gordius"), 57
Don Manley, 44–45, 74
Edward Powys Mathers ("Torquemada"), 73, 81, 134
Emily Cox, 116–117
Eric Westbrook, 168–169
Georges Perec, 45, 53, 134
Henry Rathvon, 116–117
Jerry Farrell, 62, 64–65, 177
John Graham ("Araucaria"), 87–88, 150–152
John Henderson ("Enigmatist"), 98
John Lampkin, 48
Kathryn Friedlander, 98–99, 101–102
Leonard Berstein, 77
Leonard Dawe, 130–131
Lewis Carroll, 36–37, 39
Matt Ginsberg, 119–120
Merl Reagle, 141–144, 148–149
Mudd, 83, 86
Notabili, 83
Orlando, 82, 85, 166
Patrick Berry, 68
Paul, 74, 81, 85, 87
Philip Fine, 98
Puck, 83
Quixote, 85
Roger Squires ("Rufus"), 80, 87, 123
Ruth Crisp ("Crispa"), 123
Steven Sondheim, 77
Tom Driberg ("Tiresias"), 149
Tracy Gray, 170–171
Viking, 86
Virgilius, 81
whodunit mystery writers, 135–138
Crossworder's Own Newsletter (Newman), 56
Crosswordese/crosswordiness, 43–45
"Crossword Mama You're Puzzling Me" (song), 14
"Cross Word Papa (You Sure Puzzle Me)" (song), 14
Crossword puzzles. *See also* Technology, crosswording and
about origin of the name, 7
appearance of first puzzle, ix, 162
Arthur Wynne and beginning of, 28, 162
best puzzle of 21st Century, 139
creation of jargon, 20–21
development as American fad, 13–14, 154
development as British fad, 14–19
favorite crosswordy words, 45–48
judging difficulty and good taste, 147–152
learning the art, 115

Crossword puzzles (*cont.*)
  "New Wave" movement, 56–57
  patenting idea, 11–12
  publishing first book, 8–10
  rules over cheating, 91–96
"Cross Words Between My Sweetie and Me" (song), 13–14
Crossword solvers
  assumptions and expectations of, 164–165
  cheating, rules about, 91–96
  computers as, 118–121
  depiction as "oddballs" and "loners," 116–117
  depiction in TV and movies, 52–53, 109–112, 114, 116, 139–144
  determining character and personality of, 172–173
  discovering new words, 45
  drug use by, 58
  proving constructor wrong, 145–146
  reaching "penny-drop" moment, x, 98–99, 143, 151
  replacement of print, 165–169
  research on cognitive skills, 97–102
  resources for, 175–178
  tournaments and timed play tips, 74–75, 103–108, 140
Crossword solvers (identified solutionists)
  Al Sanders, 103–104, 106
  Aric Egmont, 116–117
  I. Cresswell, 77
  John Gielgud, 95–96
  Jon Stewart, 103–104
  Marc Romano, 104, 107, 113–114
  Mark Goodliffe, 105–106
  Meredith Gardner, 125–126
  Mike Mussina, 103–104, 115
  Nitsuh Abebe, 144
  Peter Biddlecombe, 107
  Peter Brooksbank, 105
  P. G. Wodehouse, 153–154
  Rosalind Runcie, 150
  Stanley Sedgewick, 128
Crossword solvers (notable solutionists)
  Bill Clinton, 103–104
  Christopher Robin, 160
  Elizabeth II (queen of England), 161
  Frank Sinatra, 160
  George VI (king of England), 161
  Indira Gandhi, 160–161
  Margaret (princess), 161
  Norman Mailer, 161
  Thomas Keneally, 161
Crossworld: One Man's Journey into America's Crossword Obsession (Romano), 104, 113–114
Cruciverbalism: A Crossword Fanatic's Guide to Life in the Grid (Newman), 177
Cryptanalysis (code-breaking), 125–132
Cryptarithm (aka alphametic), 12
Cryptic crossword (puzzle variant)
  appearance of British mutation, x–xi
  detrimental effects, 99
  intelligence level and class distinction, 61–62
  Mathers as creator, 73, 81
  role of "clue," 21
  ruse of "muse," 47
  Sondheim as creator, 77–78
  use of acrostic, 24–25
  wartime code-breaking and, 125–126
Cryptic definition clues, 81–82
Cryptolog (magazine), 125
The Curious History of the Crosswords: 100 Puzzles from Then and Now (Tausig), 177
Cynewulf (Anglo-Saxon poet), 25

Daily Sketch (newspaper), 17
Danesi, Marcel, 25, 177
Dawe, Leonard, 130–131
Dawson, George Geoffrey, 50
"DE," ambiguity of words ending in, 41

Dean, Roy, 161
Deductive reasoning, 172–173
Dementia, staving off the onset, x, 97–102, 158
Dexter, Colin, 137
Didion, Joan, 62
Digital online puzzles, 106
Dodimead, David, 95
Dole, Robert, 63–65, 67
Double acrostics (puzzle), 7, 21–25, 32, 86, 134, 144
Double definition clues, 80
Down
  book section defined, xi
  creating numbering system, 11
  origin of jargon, 20–21
Drayton, Michael, 21
Dr. Fill (crossword bot), 119–121
Driberg, Tom ("Tiresias"), 149
Dr. Phil (TV show), 119
Duchamp, Marcel, 71

Egmont, Aric, 116–117
Eliot, T. S., 77
Elizabeth II (queen of England), 161
English History 1914–1915 (Taylor), 134
English language
  about making game of, ix
  adaptation to other languages, 49–51
  exploiting ambiguity of, 40–42
  favorite crosswordy words, 45–48
  lending itself to crosswordiness, 43–45
  The Simpsons' contributions, 140
  spoonerisms, origins of, 68–71
  spoonerisms, use in writings and puzzles, 71–75
  translating clues to other languages, 52–55
The Enigma (magazine), 73–74
Enigmatical Propositions, 163–164
"ER," ambiguity of words ending in, 40–41
Esperanto (artificial language), 7
Espionage. *See also* Hidden answers/messages
  crosswording as tool, x
  intelligence-gathering by CIA, 131–132
  WWII code-breaking and cryptanalysis, 125–131
Étienne, Luc, 71, 177
"Eye-Witnesses Should Not Do Cryptic Crosswords Prior to Identity Parades" (Lewis), 99

Farrar, John C., 10
Farrar, Margaret Petherbridge, 8–11, 145–146, 148
Farrar, Straus and Giroux (publisher), 11
Farrell, Jerry, 62, 64–65, 177
"The Fascinating Problem of Uncle Meleager's Will" (Sayer), 136
Fifteensquared (crossword blog), 175
Financial Times, 34, 61–62
Fine, Philip, 98
Fitzgerald, F. Scott, 59
Flippant, Peter, 34
French language, crosswordy words, 45
French, Ronald, 130–131
The Freshman (movie), 114
Friedlander, Kathryn, 98–99, 101–102
Friends (TV series), 91
Fry, Stephen, 58, 105
Fuller, Vincent, 137
FUN
  crossword puzzles as, ix–xi
  inclusion in first "Word-Cross" puzzle, 7
Future developments and advances. *See* Technology, crosswording and

Games (magazine), 65
Gandhi, Indira, 160–161

Gardner, Meredith, 125–126
Garland, John, 137
Gee, Johnny, 177
George VI (king of England), 161
Getting Away with Murder (stage play, Sondheim), 135
Gielgud, John, 95–96
Gilbert, Val, 131
Ginis, Kathleen Martin, 100
Ginsberg, Matt, 119–120
Goodliffe, Mark, 105–106
Google Goggles (software), 118
Gower Street dialect (aka spoonerism, "gowerism"), 69–70
Graham, John ("Araucaria"), 87–88, 150–152
Gray, Tracy, 170–171
Greer, Brian, 83
Grid. *See also* Crossword construction
  adaptation to other languages, 49–51
  aesthetics and parameters, 11
  appearance of, 20–21, 164
  as basic unit of crossword, 31
  computer-generated puzzles, 121–124
  finding the ninas, 30–35
  inductive reasoning and, 172–173
  letter counts in language translations, 52–55
  multi-dimensional formats, 169–171
  pay-to-play puzzles, 17–18
  use of "crosswordy" words, 43–45
Groening, Matt, 141–142
The Guardian, 32, 57, 98, 147, 150, 175

Hall, Barbara, 121
Harvard University, 14
Harvey, Georgina, 177
Hearst, William Randolph, 4
Helmlé, Eugen, 53
Henderson, John ("Enigmatist"), 98
Hidden answers/messages. *See also* Espionage
  creating cryptic clues, 79–88
  creating themed entries, 116–117, 140–144
  reaching the "penny-drop" moment, 98–99
  translations into other languages, 52–55
  use of acrostics, 22–27
  use of a nina, 30–35
  use of palindrome, 27–29
"High Stakes" (Wodehouse), 155
Hirschfeld, Al, 30
Hirschfeld, Nina, 30
The History of "Punch" (Spielmann), 24
Hollinghurst, Alan, 95
"Homer and Lisa Exchange Cross Words" (TV show), 139–144
Homer Simpson (fictional TV character), 139–144
Hook, Henry, 33
"Hooray! Hooray! Hooray! *The Cross-Word Puzzle Book* is out today" (Adams), 9
Hot Fuzz (movie), 142
Hotten, John, 69
Hot Water (Wodehouse), 156
"How to Do a Real Crossword Puzzle . . ." (Sondheim), 77
Humpty Dumpty, 39

Ido (artificial language), 7
The Illustrated London News, 24
Inductive reasoning, 172–173
Inspector Morse (TV series), 133, 137–138, 177
Interlocking words/squares, 11, 49, 80, 95, 163
Internet, crosswording in the Cloud, 166–167
I Say Nothing (Balfour), 175–176

INDEX

J

James, M. R., 157
Jargon. *See also* Across; Clue(s); Down; Grid
  about origins of, 20–21
  creating ninas, 30–35
Jed Bartlet (fictional TV character), 52–53, 84
Jigsaw puzzles, 133
Johnson, Boris, 123
Journal of Experimental Psychology, 100

K

Keneally, Thomas, 161
Klein bottle, 169

L

La Littérature Potentielle: Créations, Re-créations, Récréations (Oulipo), 177
Lampkin, John, 48
Lang, Matheson, 16–17
Larkin, Philip, 77
L'Art Du Contrepet (Étienne), 177
The Last of Sheila (Sondheim), 135
La Vie mode d'emploi [*Life: A User's Manual*] (Perec), 53, 55, 134
Le Livre Du Courage Et De La Peur (Renault), 177
Leo McGarry (fictional TV character), 146
Le Point (newspaper), 134
Les Mots croisés, procédés de considérations de l'auteur sur l'art et la manière de croiser les mots (Perec), 45, 176
Life: A User's Manual [*La Vie mode d'emploi*] (Perec), 53, 55, 134
The Listener (newspaper), 18, 76–78, 138, 169–170
Little Ramblers (musical group), 14
London *The Daily Telegraph*, 18, 123, 127, 129–131, 149
London *The Sunday Telegraph*, 84–85
London *Times*
  Adrian Bell as first constructor, 38
  Barbara Hall as puzzle editor, 121
  Crossword Championship, 34, 104–105, 150
  crossword first appearance, 18–19, 77–78
  crosswords as menace, 14–17
  George Dawson as puzzle editor, 50
  house style for puzzles, 33–34
  puzzle adaptations to technology, 166–167, 169
  Wodehouse as puzzle addict, 154–158
The Long Green Gaze: A Crossword Puzzle Mystery (Fuller), 137
Lord of the Rings trilogy (Tolkien), 34
Los Angeles Reader (newspaper), 141
Lottery, pay-to-play puzzles as, 17–18
Love of language, crossword puzzles as, ix

M

Mackail, Denis, 158
Made-up language, 7, 34
Mailer, Norman, 161
Maleska, Eugene T., 33, 46, 56–58, 65
Manley, Don, 44–45, 74
Margaret (princess of England), 161
Marital relationships, crosswording and, 52–53, 109–112, 116–117
"Marrowskies" (aka spoonerisms), 69–70
Mathers, Edward Powys ("Torquemada"), 73, 81, 134
Mazes (puzzle format), 4, 21
McElveen, George (Rev.), 14
McGraw, Phil, 119
Mental health, crosswording and, 97–102
Merrell, Patrick, 65
MI5 (British intelligence service), 129–131
Miles, Josie, 14
Millington, Roger, 176

Milne, A. A., 160
Mnemonics, 132. *See also* Acrostics (puzzle)
Möbius strip, 169
Monk (constructor), 34
Moor, Edward, 48
Moseley, David ("Gordius"), 57, 58
Mudd (constructor), 83, 86
Murder Across and Down (Resnicow), 137
"Murder Mystery" (puzzle), 135
Mussina, Mike, 103–104, 115

Nabokov, Vladimir, 24
Nader, Ralph, 63–64
Names, ambiguity of misleading, 41–42
The Nation, 88
National Security Agency (NSA), 125
The Neighbor's Home Mail (newspaper), 162–164
Newman, Stanley, 56–57, 122, 177
Newsday (magazine), 56
News of the World (newspaper), 17, 31
New Wave crosswording ("the Newman ripple"), 56–57
New York Post (newspaper), 4
The New York Times
  cryptic puzzles, 88
  Eugene Maleska as puzzle editor, 33, 46, 56–58, 65
  maintaining good taste, 148–149
  Margaret Farrar as first crossword editor, 11
  overlapping puzzle with *The Simpsons*, 139–144
  puzzles expressing political views, 63–65
  puzzles using slang, 58–59
  reporting on faked Spoonerisms, 70
  Will Shortz as puzzle editor, 57, 107, 139–141, 146–147
  Will Weng as puzzle editor, 95
  Wordplay blog, 177
New York *World* (newspaper), 4–5, 8–9, 11, 162
Ninas, 30–35
Notabili (constructor), 83
Nottingham Evening Post, 16

Obesity, crosswording and, 100
Oddities and Curiosities of Words and Literature (Bombaugh), 177
Old Testament (The Bible), 25
Olsher, Dean, 176
O'Malley, Christine, 176
Orlando (constructor), 82, 85, 166
Oulipo (Ouvroir de Littérature Potentielle), 71
The Oxford Book of English Verse, 111
The Oxford Dictionary of Quotations, 70
Oxford Guide To World Games (Augarde), 176

Palindrome, 26–28
Papalia & His Orchestra (musical group), 14
Paul (constructor), 74, 81, 85, 87
Pay-to-play puzzles, 17–18
Pearson's Magazine, 14
"Penny-drop" moment of clarity, x, 98–99, 143, 151
The People (newspaper), 17
Perception (journal), 99
Perec, Georges, 45, 53, 134
Perkin, John, 57
Perot, Ross, 63–64
Personality, crosswording and, 172–173
Petherbridge, Margaret. *See* Farrar, Margaret Petherbridge
Plaza Publishing (alias for Simon & Schuster), 8

Poe, Edgar Allen, 24, 134
Politics, crosswording and, 31–32, 63–65, 87–88
Predictions, crosswords making, 63–67
"Predictors of Crossword Puzzle Proficiency and Moderators of Age-Cognition Relations" (Hambrick), 100
Pretty Girl in Crimson Rose (Balfour), 175–176
Private Eye (magazine), 149
Prostitution, crosswording and, 87–88
Puck (constructor), 83
Pulitzer, Joseph, 4
The Puzzle Instinct: The Meaning of Puzzles in Human Life (Danesi), 177
Puzzles of 1925 (musical revue), 13

Quigley, Brendan Emmett, 32, 58, 79, 114
Quixote (constructor), 85

Rathvon, Henry, 116–117
Reagan, Ronald, 65
Reagle, Merl, 141–144, 148–149
Rebuse (puzzle format), 4
Renault, Gilbert (aka Colonel Rémy), 72, 177
Resnicow, Herbert, 137
Reversal clues, 84–85
Rhombus (puzzle format), 12
Ritchie, A. F. ("Arfit"), 37–39, 83–84, 177
Robin, Christopher, 160
Romano, Marc, 104, 107, 113–114
Rosenberg, Julius and Ethel, 125–126
Rubicon (TV series), 142
Rubik's Cube, 169
Run-DMC (music group), 59
Runny Babbit: A Billy Sook (Silverstein), 68

Sanders, Al, 104, 106
Sartre, Jean-Paul, 126
Sayer, Dorothy L., 136–137
Schuster, M. Lincoln ("Max"), 8
Schwed, Peter, 177
Secret messages. *See* Espionage; Hidden answers/messages
Sedgewick, Stanley, 128
75 Years of the Times *Crossword*, 175
Sex, crosswording and, 87, 150
Shirley (Brontë), 21
Shortz, Will, 57, 63, 64–65, 107, 139–141, 146–147
Sideways (movie), 109
The Silent World of Nicholas Quinn (Dexter), 138
Silverstein, Shel, 68
Simon & Schuster, Inc. (publisher), 8–10
Simon, Richard L. ("Dick"), 8
The Simpsons (TV series), x, 6–7, 139–144
Sinatra, Frank, 160
A Six-Letter Word for Death (Moyes), 137
Smith, Michael, 177
Solutionists, 11
Something Fishy (Wodehouse), 159
Sondheim, Stephen, 76–78, 125, 135
Soundalike clues, 85–86
"Sound Thinking" (game), 167
The Spectator (newspaper), 18
Spielmann, Marion, 24
Spooner, Archibald ["the Spoo"] (Rev.), 69–70, 74
Spoonergram, 73–74
Spoonerisms, 7, 68–75
Spying. *See* Espionage
From Square One: A Meditation, with Digressions, on Crosswords (Olsher), 176

Squires, Roger ("Rufus"), 80, 87, 123
Station X: The Codebreakers of Bletchley Park (Smith), 177
Stenography, 8
Stewart, Jon, 103–104
"Sticky Wickets at Blandings" (Wodehouse), 158
Still Life (stage play), 109
The Strand Magazine, 155
The Strange World of the Crossword (Millington), 176
Sudokus, 51, 100, 101, 167
Suffolk Words and Phrases: or, An Attempt to Collect the Lingual Localisms of That County (Moor), 48
Sugarhill Gang (music group), 59
Summer Moonshine (Wodehouse), 153–154
Sunday Graphic (newspaper), 17
The Swimming-Pool Library (Hollinghurst), 95
Sybil (Erythraean prophetess), 24
Synonyms, 15–16, 51, 58, 85–86, 93, 101, 121

Tabourot, Étienne, 26
Tamsworth Herald, 15
Tausig, Ben, 177
Taylor, A. J. P., 134
Teamwork/team spirit, crosswording and, 114–116
Technology, crosswording and
- about future of, 164–168
- crossword construction, 121–124
- crossword solving, 119–121
- digital online puzzles, 106
- multi-dimensional formats, 169–171
- replacement of print, 168–169
- sudoku-solving, 118–119
- wartime code-breaking, 128–129

"*Telegraph* Six," 123
Telekinesis puzzle, 62, 66, 178
"The Riddler: Meet the Marquis de Sade of the Puzzle World" (Jerz), 177
With This Puzzle, I Thee Kill (Hall), 137
Times Crossword Championship, 34, 104–105, 150
Times for the Times (crossword blog), 175
Timeshift: How to Solve a Cryptic Crossword (film documentary), 177
"Tlön, Uqbar, Orbis Tertius" (Borges), 55
Tolkien, J. R. R., 34
The Torquemada Puzzle Book (Mathers), 73
Tournaments and Championships
- American Crossword Puzzle Tournament, 74–75, 103–104, 106–108, 119–121
- "Citywide Crossword Tournament," 140
- *Times* Crossword Championship, 34, 104–105, 150
- U.S. Open Crossword Puzzle Championship, 167

Translations
- differing letter counts, 52–55
- multiple meanings of English words, 49–51

"The Truth About George" (Wodehouse), 155
Turning the Pages: An Insider's Story of Simon & Schuster 1924–1984 (Schwed), 177
The Two Ronnies (TV show), 73

U.S. Open Crossword Puzzle Championship, 167

"The Vane Sisters" (Nabokov), 24
Veltman, Noah, 43–44

The Victorians (Wilson), 134
Victoria (queen of England), 22–23
Virgilius (constructor), 81
Vowels
as nicknames, slang, and formulas, 58
words starting and ending with, 43–44, 46
words without, 47

The Wall Street Journal, 88
Weng, Will, 95
Westbrook, Eric, 168–169
West Side Story (Broadway musical), 76
The West Wing (TV series), x, 52–53, 146
Wheen, Francis, 149
White, F. D., 11
Whodunit mystery novels, crosswords and, 133–138
Why Didn't They Ask Evans? (Christie), 136
Wilson, A. N., 134
Wodehouse, P. G. ("Plum"), 46, 148, 153–159
Woolf, Virginia, 77
"Word-Cross," 7, 28, 162
Word diamond (puzzle format), 28
Wordplay (film documentary), 103–104, 106, 115, 139, 176
Wordplay (*New York Times* blog), 141–142, 177
Word search (puzzle format), 4, 51
Word square (puzzle format), 4–6, 27–29
Workshop of Potential Literature (Oulipo), 71
The World (newspaper), 4–5, 8–9, 11, 162
World War I, 20, 127
World War II, 125–131, 157–158
Wynne, Arthur
about origins of "Word-Cross," 3–7, 28, 162
failure to patent idea, 11–12
solution to first puzzle, 178

Yale University, 14
The Year of Magical Thinking (Didion), 62
You Have the Right to Remain Puzzled (Hall), 137

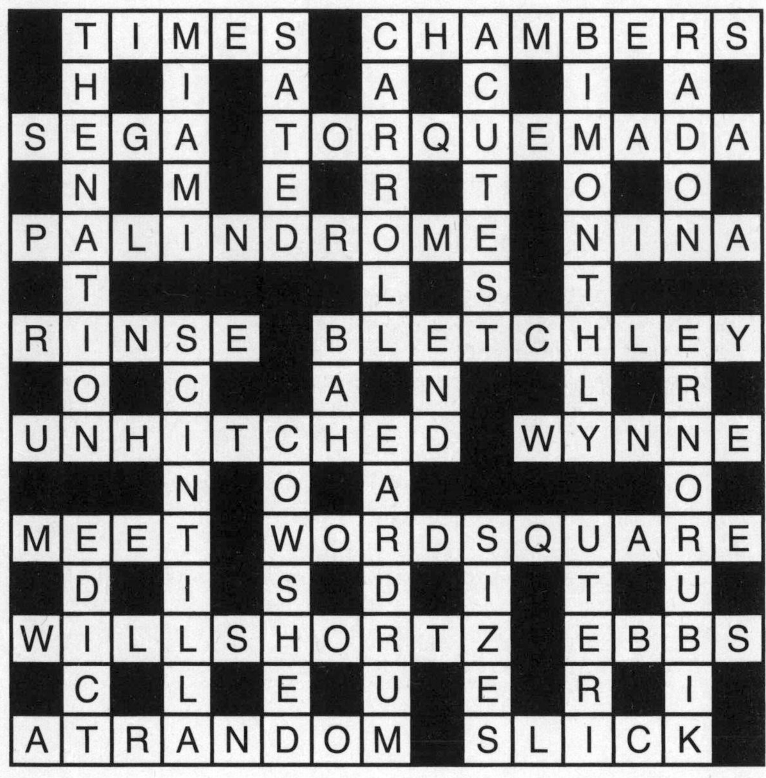

ACROSS

1. TIMES (*items* anag.) 4. CHAMBERS (2 defs.) 8. SEGA (*ages* rev.) 9. TORQUE + MAD + At 10. PALIN + D + ROME 11. N + IN + A (& lit.) 12. RI(N)SE 14. B + LETCH + LE + Y 17. pUN(HIT) CHED 20. WYNNE (hom.) 21. ME + ET 23. WO(RDSQUA)RE (*R* + *squad* anag.) 26. WILL SHORTZ (*shill warts* spoonerism) 27. E + BBS 28. AT RANDOM (*mandator* anag.) 29. S + LICK

DOWN

1. sT(HEN)ATION 2. MI + A + MI 3. SATED (first and last letter swap in DATES) 4. CARROLL (hom.) 5. AC(UTES)T 6. BIMONTHLY (*BLT, hominy* anag.) 7. RAD + ON 13. SC(INT) ILLA 14. BlAH 15. bEND 16. ERNO RUBIK (*I broke urn* anag.) 18. CrOW(SHE)D 19. EARDRUM (*murder a* anag.) 22. EDICT (*cited* anag.) 24. SeIZES 25. UTERI (hid.)

Puzzle by Brendan Emmett Quigley